Reconciliation of Worship in the Black Church

Spontaneous Worship

Charles E. Lewis Sr.

iUniverse, Inc.
Bloomington

Reconciliation of Worship in the Black Church
Spontaneous Worship

iUniverse books may be ordered through booksellers or by contacting:

iUniverse
1663 Liberty Drive
Bloomington, IN 47403
www.iuniverse.com
1-800-Authors (1-800-288-4677)

ISBN: 978-1-4502-9827-8 (sc)
ISBN: 978-1-4502-9829-2 (dj)
ISBN: 978-1-4502-9828-5 (ebk)

Printed in the United States of America

iUniverse rev. date: 2/28/2011

Contents

Dedication

This book is dedicated to the memory of my parents, Rev. James William Lewis and Evangelist Eva Mae Lewis. They carried me to church without fail as a child, even when I had no desire to attend any type of church service.

Without the lifelong sacrifices my parents made, none of my past, present, or future accomplishments would be possible. As a pastor my father demonstrated what true love and concern for God's people really is. And from his example I've learned that it's love that truly makes the difference in anyone's life, because his love for me made a difference in my life.

Acknowledgments

It is impossible to complete a work of this scope without support of all kinds—academic, emotional, spiritual, practical, and financial—from many people. In fact, all the pages of this book would not be enough to contain the expressions of thanks that are due each and every person who contributed in some way to bring this work to completion.

I want to thank Dave Currie, director of the Doctor of Ministry program at Gordon-Conwell Theological Seminary. This work was originally presented to the faculty of Gordon-Conwell as a Doctor of Ministry thesis, and Dave served as my mentor. To Bishop Ralph Love Sr., the Presiding Prelate of the Southern District Convocation of the United Holy Church of America, I offer my thanks for allowing me to pass out the surveys during our annual convocation. Thanks also is due Bishop Elijah Williams, President of the United Holy Church of America, for being my first survey participant.

I thank the students at United Christian College of Goldsboro, North Carolina, for taking the survey and helping me analyze the data received from all the surveys taken; and the chaplaincy training in clinical pastoral education (CPE) at Pitt Memorial Hospital, which enhanced my understanding of the relationship between worship, pastoral care, and the psychotherapeutic disciplines.

Thanks, also, to the members of the churches I pastor, Antioch United Holy Church and Kairos Church Ministry, for all the support and love during this process. You are all treasures!

Finally, my deepest love, passion, and devotion must be expressed to my wife of twenty-eight years, Mrs. Lisa M. Lewis. Her affection and good humor, along with the continual giggly smiles of my son and daughters, Charles Jr., Nicole, and Barbara, never fail to energize me, providing the determination, strength, and joy to persevere and to be my best.

Introduction

One of the basic features of church life in the black church is the proliferation of worship and music. The purpose of this study is to aid in the revitalization and restoration of worship within the black church so that a practical theology of worship can be developed, incorporating traditional devotional-style worship and contemporary-style praise and worship. While I address this issue through a study of my own denomination, the United Holy Church of America (UHC), it is my hope that the black church as a whole will benefit as well.

The project begins with identification of the two types of worship: traditional devotional-style worship, with its focus on spontaneous worship, and contemporary praise and worship, with its emphasis on a rehearsed worship.

The project will look at the historical backdrop of the devotional service, which has been a major part of the United Holy Church since its inception. The genesis of the United Holy Church will be explored to view the paths of devotional-style, or spontaneous worship. Worshipers' views of the worship styles of the local church will be explored through a written survey administered by the author to different congregants.

The content of this project involves identifying the problem and its setting and presenting a theological framework, literature review, methodology of research, and outcome of the project. This project also will demonstrate the need to embrace both styles of worship with the hope of revitalizing worship so that believers and seekers will sense a real worship experience.

Chapter 1

THE PROBLEM

> "Unless people have a pride in themselves, how are they to liberate themselves?"
>
> David Dargie[1]

The first thing that truly helped me focus on this subject was a lesson taught by Dr. Gary Parrett, one of my instructors at Gordon-Conwell Theological Seminary. He stated, "The idea of this course is that we learn to be 'culturally relevant,' 'biblically faithful,' and to be responsive to the gospel and culture."[2] This opened a whole new perspective in my thinking, for I saw that the blending of worship styles is not the only thing that is important; being true to who you are is just as important, not only to yourself but also to God. The providence of God holds true in every aspect of life, and if our culture and style of worship were good enough for Him to reach down and save us in that culture, then we must be true to the setting in which God has placed us.

Missionaries like the Quakers and Methodists encountered the early African tribes and interrupted the setting, delivering to the black church ill-fitting garments, that is, a style of worship

---

1   David Dargie "African Church Music and Liberation" (Durban: University of Natal, September 16, 1982), 11.
2   Gary Parrett, "Culturally Relevant" (D.Min. course notes, Gordon-Conwell Theological Seminary, May 2008).

that did not fit. Those missionaries brought a Western religion that was not tailored to the black church. I find today that in some African American churches members are still trying to embrace a garment that does not fit. This is mostly because we have not taken the time to become comfortable with our own garments. We continue to embrace the old saying that "the grass looks greener in someone else's pasture." Another cliché that has hampered African American people for a number of years in so many aspects of life is that "Mr. Charlie's ice is colder," suggesting the possibility that what white Christianity offers is better than what African Americans have within the black church.

The culture of the black church tradition emphasizes that personal conviction, moral renewal, and sanctification should manifest themselves in acts of justice, charity, triumphant singing, and service in the wider world. Singing sets the stage or mood by preparing the audience emotionally and physically for the preacher, whose communication task is made easier because of the audience's receptivity. Singing soothes the emotions and draws the congregation together; therefore, the preacher often inherits an attentive audience by virtue of the choir or praise team. Maynard-Reid states that "worship practices are as culturally conditioned as any other aspect of human experience."[3] He maintains that "what we perceive as appropriate worship is culturally conditioned and has little to do with Biblical orthodoxy or soteriological morality."

Maynard-Reid writes, "If worship does not have its grounding in people's lives and cultural experiences, it will remain foreign, imposed and irrelevant."[4] This is especially true within African American culture, because it is rooted and grounded in an experience very much like the Exodus, when God delivered a nation that was oppressed and held in captivity. This identification

---

3   Pedrito U. Maynard-Reid, *Diverse Worship: African-American, Caribbean & Hispanic Perspectives* (Downers Grove, IL: InterVarsity, 2000), 60-61.

4   Maynard-Reid, *Diverse Worship*, 63.

with Israel's oppression at the hands of the Egyptians causes the African American culture to relate to the scriptural text of bondage and freedom.

Freedom is a very important aspect of the African American cultural context. African American Christianity has sought this freedom throughout the generations of Western religion. This pursuit at times has led some to give up their own culture to follow that of the Western society. It is the author's hope through this work that the black church learns to be culturally relevant without being culturally defiant.

The significant challenge within the author's faith community is the blending of our traditional style with what has been titled in the late twentieth and early twenty-first centuries as praise and worship. This particular platform has caused some uneasiness within the author's faith community because it is said to be entertaining and not true worship or praise. Also, the title itself has caused some apprehension among the leaders within the United Holy Church faith community. Therefore, blending the concept of praise and worship with our traditional, devotional-style worship, which is totally spontaneous, has truly birthed a division within the community.

The twenty-first century has also seen the development of drama worship with praise dancers or liturgical dance, mime ministry, youth step team, and drama skits. All of this has caused some restlessness within the Holiness-Pentecostal movements, including in the United Holy Church of America. The focus of this particular work, however, is examining both devotional worship and praise and worship to determine whether they can be considered biblical worship and whether they can be blended so that both groups can come together.

What is biblical worship? Biblical worship is worship in spirit and truth, which means according to the Word of God and with a heart full of love for God. Biblical worship is offered through the Lord Jesus Christ as the only mediator who stands in the congregation and declares God's name to His people and sings God's praises with His people – praises that include the diverse songs of all nations, all generations, and all socioeconomic classes.

Biblical worship is Christ-centered and gospel-centered, as people from every tribe and tongue and language and nation sing praise to the Lamb who was slain for the sins of the world. Biblical worship is Word-centered in all the elements of prayer, reading of Scripture, preaching, confessions of faith, offerings, singing of psalms, hymns, and spiritual songs, and the sacraments. Biblical worship makes use of the gifts of God's people under the wise oversight and leadership of qualified and trained leaders. These are overarching biblical principles by which to evaluate true worship.

Biblical worship additionally carries with it the instruments of biblical songs, as in the celebrated days of David, when four thousand Levites were appointed as full-time musicians to assist in worship, using wind instruments, stringed instruments, and percussive instruments. This innovative style of worship both fulfills those days and anticipates the even greater glories of eternal, heavenly worship. In Revelation, John provides images of what worship is like in heaven and, as many Pentecostals believe, what it will be like after the rapture of the church.

> Then I looked, and I heard around the throne and the living creatures and the elders the voice of many angels, numbering myriads of myriads and thousands of thousands, saying with a loud voice, "Worthy is the Lamb who was slain, to receive power and wealth and wisdom and might and honor and glory and blessing!" And I heard every creature in heaven and on earth and under the earth and in the sea, and all therein, saying, "To him who sits upon the throne and to the Lamb be blessing and honor and glory and might forever and ever!" And the four living creatures said,

"Amen!" and the elders fell down and worshiped.
(Rev 5:11-14 RSV)

The images John presents are of worshipers giving animated, enthusiastic praise before the throne of God night and day. Indeed, all of creation (in heaven, on earth, under the earth, and in the sea) is in motion and is pictured as joyously praising God. The Revelation passage calls to mind imagery from Isaiah: "The mountains and hills before you shall break forth into singing and all the trees of the field shall clap their hands" (55:12 RSV).

Worship is the gospel in motion. This is an awesome view of worship because worship is the gospel enacted, which is the powerful view of worship presented by Isaiah and John in Revelation. Looking at the devotional-style worship in the United Holy Church and other black denominations versus the modern-day praise and worship style calls for a compromise, or what Robert Webber calls a "blend of worship, which brings the traditional and contemporary together in creative ways."[5] This concept of blended worship allows believers to learn from traditions other than our own, as well as to incorporate new worship ideas. It also allows us to see its commitment to the Scriptures as the foundation for worship. Moreover, it delivers the view that worship is not a human invention but a God-given gift. Implementing this truth is of paramount importance. James Cone, in "Sanctification, Liberation, and Black Worship,"[6] offers great help in speaking about characteristics of black worship. He outlines six principal components of black worship: preaching, singing, shouting, conversion, prayer, and testimony. For Cone, "song in the black worship experience opens the people's hearts for God's Spirit and intensifies the power of the Spirit's presence."[7]

---

5   Robert E. Webber, *Planning Blended Worship: The Creative Mixture of Old and New* (Nashville: Abingdon, 1998), 59.

6   James H. Cone, "Sanctification, Liberation, and Black Worship," *Theology Today* (July 1978): 139-40.

7   Cone, "Sanctification, Liberation, and Black Worship," 152.

Black worship is participative, as seen through the informal "call and response" between minister and worshipers. But also through testifying (another term encountered in Cone's work), people relate to one another and relate the faith to life, thus edifying (or spiritually building up) all present. It is clear from the testimonies and other elements of worship that the members have a heavy emotional investment in one another.

The problem that rests at the door of the UHC is that its focus on devotional service in the churches of the Southern District Convocation of the United Holy Church of America brings to the surface the need for implementing a blending of styles of worship, particularly the traditional style with the contemporary praise and worship style. One of the basic features of church life in the United Holy Church is the proliferation of worship and music, which is captured through the spontaneous type worship. This type of worship has caused many severe conflicts both within individual congregations in the UHC and within the whole denomination. Having grown up in the UHC, I see most worship in the UHC falling within the two broad categories of contemporary worship and historic, devotional-style worship.

My father, the late Rev. James W. Lewis, Sr., carried me to church as a child. I recall within the grand church the spontaneity and Spirit-filled atmosphere of Sunday morning testimony services, where the saints of God would jump to their feet one after another and speak about the goodness of God in their lives. This type of spontaneous worship was sometimes the highlight of the worship service because not only would people testify of God's goodness, but they also would dance in the Spirit under open heavens. As the years have gone by, devotional-style worship, or spontaneous worship, has come to be thought of as just a bunch of noise. Yet, this type of religious experience and expression supported the beliefs of the early believers. They also felt that this form of worship was a part of their heritage and would be passed on to the next generation.

The spontaneity of tongues, songs, and dancing was and is the energy of the UHC worship experience. Worship in the UHC is in need of revitalization; however, this does not mean that UHC worshipers must abandon their worship style, but rather, that they incorporate some much-needed change. The worship style of the UHC has always been the spontaneous style of worship; however, we need to blend some of the new with the old. Over the years we have lost that old style because churches have totally disposed of the devotional-style worship, which has identified us as a black charismatic Holiness/Pentecostal group. The UHC went through a major separation in 1977. This separation kept the UHC torn apart for over twenty years. What appeared to be reconciliation took place with these two frayed entities in May 2000; however the worship styles appear to still be in need of reconciliation.

It appears that more time is spent on things that do not lead to worship or to reconciliation of hearts. Therefore, pastors within UHC churches (discussed in chapter four) feel that congregations are bleeding, and life is slowly draining from them as they try to find who they are and what they should be doing. There is a need for a careful, theological worship statement within our churches. The purpose of this theological enterprise will be to discern clearly the nature of worship in order to understand more adequately who UHC are as worshipers.

Norma Malefyt and Howard Vanderwell, in *Designing Worship Together,* state that "every congregation need a standard, statement written down so that all can refer to it."[8] Each congregation has enough conflicting opinions and preferences to create unsettling confusion unless those who lead provide clear direction with "a clear statement of the theology of worship that guides the congregation and that does so in language and concepts that a layperson can understand."[9]

---

8   Norma deWaal Malefyt and Howard Vanderwell, *Designing Worship Together: Models and Strategies for Worship Planning* (Herndon, VA: The Alban Institute, 2005), 69.

9   Malefyt and Vanderwell, *Designing Worship Together,* 71.

Sculptor Josefina de Vasconcellos's work entitled "Reconciliation" originally was named "Reunion."[10] This sculpture depicts a man and woman embracing each other across barbed wire. This sculpture commemorates the end of the Second World War in Europe, which separated families for years.

Josefina de Vasconcellos's Reunion

The idea for this sculpture came from the story of a woman who crossed Europe on foot to find her husband. As I read about this work of art and viewed the actual monument erected for the cause of "reconciliation," it reminded me of the UHC, because believers are worshiping together but are not reconciled. Often the body of Christ gives the appearance of being united because worshipers have traveled many miles to come together; however, they are still embracing through barbed wire. We must remove this wire that hinders true community worship. Removal will allow the church to totally reconcile and revitalize our form of worship so that the power and strength that was once known in

10   http://www.know-britain.com/churches/images/coventry_cathedral_
reconciliation_statue.html.

the UHC can return. We must understand that it is the worship experience that will release the power of God.

The UHC, as well as the wider black church, must regain the style of worship and unity that will help to stabilize a people during a period of tremendous change, because motivated worship will deliver transformation with the aid of the Holy Spirit. The church came into being in 1886, "only twenty years removed from the Civil War [when] the black presence was considered a nuisance."[11] The church was caught in a storm as society was transitioning from an agrarian past to a modern, industrial, and urban era, and it was the church's worship style that gave them strength to endure. We do not have to just shrug and accept the way we are; through the power of the indwelling Holy Spirit, true transformation and real life change is possible. This is what is behind Kierkegaard's wonderful prayer: "And now, Lord, with your help I shall become myself."[12] It is through worship, music, singing, and community that the UHC will become what God has predestined.

The strength of the music popularized by urban contemporary gospel pioneers had its roots mostly in "spiritual songs by southern slaves brought from Africa during the eighteenth and nineteenth century but also in the freewheeling forms of religious devotion of 'sanctified' or 'holiness' churches."[13] This type of singing encouraged individual church members to "testify," speaking and singing spontaneously about their faith and experience, sometimes while dancing in celebration.

This project will look at the celebration of worship that is the historical backdrop of the devotional service, which has been a major part of the UHC since its inception. This devotional service

11   William C. Turner Jr., *The United Holy Church of America* (Piscataway, NJ: Gorgias Press, 2006), 22.

12   Walter Kaufmann, *Existentialism from Dostoevsky to Sartre* (New York: New American Library, 1975), 203

13   C, Eric Lincoln and Lawrence H. Mamiya, *The Black Church in the African American Experience* (Durham: Duke University Press, 2001), 76-79.

is filled with traditional-style songs with a time for testimony from the congregants in a spontaneous-worship format. Devotional service is totally spontaneous, traditional-style worship, which includes prayer, song, dance, praise, adoration, and any form of worship responding back to the God of heaven. The contemporary style of praise and worship consists of being led into singing from a totally rehearsed group; nevertheless, it has the same ability to lead people into an open heaven with a move of the Holy Spirit.

Devotional Service

Defining "devotional service" worship is somewhat difficult because it actually has the same format as a regular Sunday morning worship service. Devotional service has a prayer, Scripture reading, and a song. Then each participant is allowed the opportunity to sing a song spontaneously or give a testimony of the goodness of God or of a trial that they experienced while walking with God during the past week or the last month. At the completion of this style of worship, the regular morning worship begins by calling the congregation together for worship and starting with a song, Scripture, and prayer. However, in "praise and worship" a team of individuals sings worship and praise songs and does not allow for individual testimony or the releasing of the spontaneity of songs. This service, however, also is opened by a prayer and Scripture reading, which then moves directly into the praise and worship phase of the service.

The UHC has practiced the devotional service to begin its worship service since the church's beginning. This concept will be evaluated to determine its biblical connection and its usefulness to our church. A survey will be taken on a voluntary basis to evaluate the views of this concept of devotional worship. The focus of the survey will analyze how the service is done and its effectiveness. The typical order during devotional time is testimonies, Scripture readings, and songs on a rotational basis; however during these devotional periods, there is no preparation, nor is it considered a part of the regular morning worship service, which is shown by the statement made at the conclusion of the devotional service, "It's time to begin morning worship." We will look to determine whether these concepts of devotion and the devotional-style worship itself are worth saving through reconciliation and revitalization in part or in whole.

The setting for this style of devotional service is primarily found within the black community, and most of the churches within the UHC are in North Carolina. It was after my first doctoral residence that I began to feel that the devotional services could be incorporated in our modern-day services. I completed a case study on this issue during a class setting, and most of my classmates felt this is an important part of our heritage and should be kept alive. Therefore, this project will explore every attempt to reclaim this part of history within the UHC community.

The history of the UHC is sewn into the Holiness/Pentecostal denominational church, which was conceived in the year of 1886. This was a predominantly black organization founded in the south on the heels of slavery. "This church was built upon the foundation of the Apostles, Prophets, and Jesus Christ Himself being the chief cornerstone. The UHC conception was one hundred years after Richard Allen and Absalom Jones had been pulled from their knees praying; one hundred years after the famous Bethel Church was begun the United Holy Church of America was born."[14]

The UHC was filled largely from the pews of the Methodist Church. There were massive revivals stretching across the lands with divine energy, and great experiences came as a result of these meetings. But the founding fathers of the UHC were pushed out of the Methodist Church because of their testimony of a Spirit-filled life. The spontaneous reaction to "the Holy Spirit was not tolerated in the Methodist Church and Elder Mason, Charles and Emma Craig were pushed out of St. Joseph African Methodist

---

14   Chester W. Gregory, *The History of the United Holy Church of America, Inc., 1886-2000* (Baltimore: Gateway Press, 2000), 1-4.

Church."[15] It became official after they refused to renounce their testimony to holiness and sanctification. This style of spontaneous worship birthed numerous churches in houses throughout their community, which was a mirroring of the book of Acts. This led to churches being established and an association being formed, where people could feel free to seek God, not only to grow in a sense of being genuinely saved, but also to be sanctified, and to express themselves through spontaneous testimonies and devotional service.

The UHC further developed its spontaneous testimonies and devotional services and Pentecostal style as a result of the Azusa Street meetings. Frank Bartleman was considered an eyewitness to the Azusa Street gatherings.[16] He stated that after the great meeting a gentleman by the name of Gaston Barnabus Cashwell of the Pentecostal Holiness Church in North Carolina returned to Dunn, North Carolina, and he was "speaking in the German tongue."[17] This man preached to the "south and led several southern holiness denominations into the Pentecostal movement and the United Holy Church of America."[18] L. M. Mason, a founder of UHC, also was present at that meeting.

Through this experience came cathartic expressivism, which is how our testimonies and devotional services were described. Often when the senses and the "human spirit are engaged in a powerful way, people feel compelled to express themselves through emotion and action which may be ineffable."[19] Shouting is often a part of the devotional services of the UHC. The term can refer to a wide range of behaviors—from the joyful ecstasy of praise to the heartrending anguish of uncensored grief—that express the worshipers' immediate sense of God's presence. Also, during designated moments of formal worship, shouters may stand, clap

15 Gregory, *The History of the United Holy Church*, 35.
16 Frank Bartleman, *Azusa Street—The Roots of Modern-day Pentecost* (Plainfield, NJ: Logos, 1980), xix.
17 Frank Bartleman, *Azusa Street* (Plainfield, NJ: Logos, 1980), 29.
18 Bartleman, *Azusa Street,* 31.
19 Bartleman, *Azusa Street,* 35-42.

their hands, walk around, dance, leap, weep, speak in tongues, kneel, hug someone, or lay prostrate on the floor in response to an overwhelming encounter with what is referred to as the awe-inspiring holiness of God. This has developed into what is seen as a liturgical accommodation to the worshiper's need and desire to encounter the holy in this personal, embodied manner, and it encourages the release of powerful energies that might otherwise be suppressed to the detriment of the person.

Devotional services also allow the expression of internal concerns in a public forum through the ritual of testifying, which was initially birthed in the small groups and reinforced during the Azusa Street meetings. This tradition has a formula that includes at least five elements. The first is an opening expression, showing respect to God and the community of elders; the second is a declaration of one's current spiritual condition; the third is an account of trials, temptations, and tribulations that have been endured in the past and present; the fourth is the individual's expression of gratitude for his or her current victorious state; and the fifth is the person request for the prayers and support of the congregation.

Another avenue of the devotional service is that of triumphant singing. This type of singing is meant to inspire hope and triumphant faith among people who are acquainted with the pain of oppression. After one finishes testifying, another will break out with a song such as "Victory Shall Be Mine," which can empower people to become fearless moral agents who struggle hopefully for a good community and a just society. This type of singing also is a therapeutic and preparatory function of black sacred music. The impressive music is accompanied by the beating of drums, guitars, washboards, tambourines, B-three organs, pianos, and any other musical instruments that can be used. I recall fellowshipping with a church where the mother of the church beat two wood blocks together, and a deacon stroked a washboard with a spoon, while another clapped the symphonic style cymbals, all keeping beat with a single bass drum beaten by another deacon. This showed musical instrument accompaniment and spontaneity at its finest. Though this type of music often involves congregational singing and is spontaneously driven, the practice seems to be a "carryover from slave culture, in which songs were generated spontaneously during work and play, and also from some West African religious cultures, where one can observe a similar creative process."[20]

Praise and Worship

The worship style that opposes the UHC devotional-style worship is that of the modern-day praise and worship. The title "praise and worship" does not clearly or accurately describe this style of worship. Rather, the title describes what the church will be doing for the next thirty or forty minutes during service time.

The end of the twentieth century gave birth to this style of worship in the charismatic church settings. Praise and worship is a popular event now in most churches, but UHC members desire to know where it came from and whether it represents a change of direction for the UHC. Many of the UHC churches adopted praise and worship after experiencing it in other churches or after attending praise conferences and viewing the megachurches through the media. The UHC congregations wrestle with one concept about praise and worship more than anything else, namely, the origin of praise and worship. The uncertainty of the origin of praise and worship creates a lack of understanding because it resembles nothing that was birthed in the UHC or that developed during the struggle. Can this style of worship be therapeutic in the lives of believers when modern-day racism strikes and the halls of justice crumble around their homes and children?

Even though music has always played a unique role in enabling people to worship, the form and presentation of praise and worship was different from anything the church had ever been involved

---

20   Gayraud S. Wilmore, *Black Religion and Black Radicalism: An Interpretation of the Religious History of African Americans* (Maryknoll, NY: Orbis, 1998), 22-23.

with before. Whether it is with our voice or with instruments, our days are to be spent praising God. Our forefathers saw fit to lay foundational truths of our faith in music. Songs like "Peace in the Valley" and "Victory in Jesus" enforce biblical teaching with praise. Praise and worship is a living and dynamic tradition, and no congregation follows any text slavishly; there are enough strands to justify a number of generalizations.

Many people think that praise and worship is simply singing songs at church, but it is so much more! It is also a condition of the heart—a willingness to exalt God and yield to His will. Worship is an expression of love and awe to the God who gives us more than we deserve. Whether we express our worship by singing, playing music, dancing, or in some other way, we must remember that we are called to worship God with our every action, every day of your lives. God is holy, loving, and worthy of all our worship and devotion.

One characteristic of praise and worship, as described and mandated in Scripture, is the tendency to be more active than Protestant worship generally has been. The notion of bowing or prostration, which is contained in the Hebrew and Greek words for worship, suggests that worship in Scripture is more physical than we often allow. The body can (must?) be more actively involved in worship. A second motif is that praise is very dominant in biblical worship, and such praise is often loud and exuberant and involves the whole congregation. Again, if our tradition is too oriented toward one set style, we must bridge our version to this biblical exuberance of adoration and praise. D.A. Carson informs us, "Christian worship embraces both adoration and action."[21] This shows that our worship in any format involves a dual method.

The quarrel, or observation, that the UHC congregations have is that the older worshipers who have sunk their teeth into devotional-style worship feel that praise and worship groups insist

---

21   D.A. Carson, ed., *Worship by the Book* (Grand Rapids: Zondervan, 2002), 43.

that "praise" and "worship" should be the chosen way of worship. Also, they express the view that in praise and worship praise occurs early in the adoration experience. We thank God especially for what He does; but our souls also are involved, and we have exuberant singing. (Devotional-style worshipers feel that these things happen from beginning to end in a devotional service.) In praise and worship, the worshipers sense that as they get into the praise more, they shift to worship. They then become focused on who God is, and then their spirits are engaged, and they may end in silent wonder. Carson states, "Worship occurs when our spirit contacts God's spirit."[22] Something sparks between God and us, and—SNAP!—we're involved in a worship experience. As the soloist (devotional-style worshipers call him or her an entertainer) begins to sing unto the Lord, that mystical "snap" occurs.

---

22   Carson, ed., *Worship by the Book,* 18-20.

Chapter 2

THEOLOGICAL AND BIBLICAL ANALYSIS
"Lift up your hands in the sanctuary and praise the Lord"

Psalm 134:2

United Holy Church General Convocation, Greensboro, North Carolina

As one analyzes the UHC theologically and biblically, the church's embracement of the African religious perspective is quite visible. Within this perspective believers see their belief imbedded in the biblical text and in the fabric of black liberation theology. Like most biblical communities, this community of faith convenes with the Lord in the very long moments of cries as they await their deliverance from their oppressor.

James Cones states,

> A very special link was forged during the bondage between the God of scripture and the African slave bereft of every other form of identify—homeland, language, religion, kinship. The African slave worshipers' new life became marked by hope and a profound trust that the God of his enslaver would bring deliverance. The Bible for the slave ancestors was both the holy book and primer; and like the African who received the Gospel from missionaries during colonialism, the new religion was a way both to salvation and to a new socio-political existence.[23]

This kind of hope, coupled with biblical principles and the leading of the Spirit of God, is the basis for the UHC churches' spontaneous style of worship. The UHC, like other African American believers, have endured social and political maltreatment. The Bible has been their source of strength and has given them the freedom to worship spontaneously. The theological concept of spontaneous worship is similar to prophetic worship. Paul said in 1 Corinthians 14:26, "So here's what I want you to do. When you gather for worship, each one of you is prepared with

---

23   James H. Cone and Gayraud S. Wilmore, eds., *Black Theology: A Documentary History Volume I 1966-1979* (Maryknoll, NY: Orbis, 1993), 185.

something that will be useful for all: Sing a hymn, teach a lesson, tell a story, lead a prayer, and provide an insight."[24]

It appears from this verse that the early church's meetings were very informal and free. There was liberty for the Spirit of God to use the various gifts He had given to the church. One man, for instance, would read a psalm, and then another would set forth some teaching. Another would speak in a foreign tongue. Another would present a revelation he had received directly from the Lord. Another would interpret the tongue that had already been given. Paul gives tacit approval to this "open meeting," where there is liberty for the Spirit of God to speak through different believers. But having stated this, he also sets forth the first constraint on the exercise of these gifts. Everything must be done with a view to edification. Just because a thing is sensational or spectacular does not mean that it has any place in the church service. In order to be acceptable, ministry must have the effect of building up the people of God. That is what is meant by edification—spiritual growth.

In the process of dealing with edification and spiritual growth, Paul has several insights into Christian worship that have application for Christians today. One principle worth noting is that of participation. The UHC devotional service truly captures this principle of participation. Paul's basic assumption is that when the congregation comes together, each person who has a gift ought to be able to exercise it; but the exercise of gifts should not be competitive or create disorder. This has been one of the downfalls of UHC devotional services, for often the testimonies appear to become very competitive. But 1 Corinthians 14:26 clearly teaches that when we gather to worship God, each of us needs to bring all of our gifts, insights, and experiences with God.

The contrast between the situation in our churches today and that in the one Paul addressed is so great as to be frightening to us. The church to which Paul wrote had no full-time staff, no

---

24 Eugene Peterson, *The Message: The Bible in Contemporary Language* (Colorado Springs: NavPress, 2002).

history of worship, and very few models to copy. They did have an exciting experience with God to celebrate and a loving fellowship to nourish, and so their worship service was sort of a spiritual "covered dish" affair in which each person brought something to be shared with the group. Paul had no problem with the idea of each person participating. While Paul felt it was counterproductive for everyone to speak at once, he never questioned the need for each Christian to participate meaningfully in worship.

This is an emphasis that desperately needs to be recaptured, because in too many instances worship has become a "spectator" activity with the focus on the contemporary praise and worship team. When each person is meaningfully involved, both the lives of the people and the quality of the worship are enriched. A service can be planned and orderly and still encourage real participation. If the needs and gifts and interests of the laity are kept in mind by those who plan the worship, then the singing of the hymns, the reading of the Scriptures, the participation in the prayers, and even the focus on the sermon together can become an event that enriches all. While this requires sensitivity to where the people are, openness to the diversity of gifts and needs, and great flexibility, it has such great potential that it is worth the effort to develop this spiritual growth within the laity.

In opposition to spontaneous worship is prepared worship, or contemporary-style praise and worship, which many feel has a lack of intimacy, purity of heart, and accessibility. Yet the current generation church believes that prepared worship has been used for millennia in responsive readings, recited prayers, and selected songs. However, spontaneous worship is the worship of David's dancing and New Testament believers falling to their knees in grateful prayer. This form of worship describes a picture of exuberance, of unrestrained joy, and of happiness that is expressed without inhibitions. Palmer states, "If theology can do something for worship, may it not also be true that worship, in its turn, can do something for theology?"[25] Job 35:10 states, "But never give

---

25   Albert W. Palmer, *The Art of Conducting Public Worship* (New York:

God a thought when things go well, when God puts spontaneous songs in their hearts.[26]

The fire of God, which comes in the midst of true Spirit-led and directed worship, will cleanse and purify all who have opened their hearts to be touched deeply by Him. All believers must face the truth that if the Holy Spirit is not allowed to touch every part of their lives and bring wholeness and purity, God has no room for their worship, and it becomes just a dead, outward form. God doesn't want us to come to Him as we think we should be but rather as we are; and if what we are is not pleasing to God and not in line with His Spirit and His Word, then we cry out for mercy to change. That is all He asks of us.

It is during spontaneous worship that we appoint the Holy Spirit as our song leader and we allow Him to direct the song service. The human song leader must be sensitive to the Holy Spirit, and then at some point He will lead us into spontaneous worship. This leads to an incredible journey of creative spontaneity and worship with such freshness that it moves like no other service. It takes total reliance on the leading of the Holy Spirit and a sensitive ear to hear His voice and the courage to follow it.

Testimonies

As we look to the biblical text, we also will find that this spontaneous style of worship is a voice for witnessing. The Bible declares that we all should be witnesses of the things of God; it employs us to tell of His goodness. One way we do this is through hymns and songs, which are a major part of devotional-style worship. The Hebrews were music-loving people. Several musical instruments, including the tambourine or timbrel, are mentioned in the Bible. Such instruments unquestionably were a major part of their devotional service. Merrymaking and music were part of their feasts and festivals. The earliest recorded song

Macmillan, 1953), 22.

26   Peterson, *The Message.*

in the Bible is referred to as the Song of Moses in Exodus 15. The Hebrews celebrated God's miraculous deliverance of them from the Egyptian army at the Red Sea by singing this hymn. Miriam took a timbrel in her hand and began to beat it joyously, dancing to its rhythm with all the people following in circles of ecstatic thanksgiving. The children of Israel celebrated God's mighty deeds. From beginning to end, it was praise of God. This correlates well with the history of the United Holy Church. The enemy dealt shrewdly with the founders of the UHC, many of whom were in bondage as sharecroppers or were made to feel they were less than men. But the members of the UHC sing spontaneously after thinking about the mighty, delivering hand of God. They celebrate God's mighty deeds with the pungent, joyous spontaneity of a delivered people rejoicing.

Spontaneous testimonies during devotional services are based upon the principle of witnessing, which is simply the giving of a testimony. Acts 14:3 states, "Long time therefore abode they speaking boldly in the Lord, which gave testimony unto word of his grace, and granted signs and wonders to be done by their hands" (KJV).

The Scripture above relates to devotional-style worship in the UHC, because Christians, and especially Christian communicators, must eventually learn how to deal with the many kinds of rejection. Paul and Barnabas's experience in Acts 14 has truly helped believers because it provides a basis for looking into the different expressions on the face of the old enemy—discouragement. It is easy to be discouraged when we see people reject devotional-style worship. But we must realize that people are complicated and their reactions are fickle. Freedom from bondage to people's responses is essential to our effectiveness in witnessing and giving our testimonies. Paul helps here because it seems probable that there were no forcible or public measures to expel Paul and Barnabas from Iconium, as there had been at Pisidian Antioch, and the apostles therefore regarded it as their duty to remain. God granted them great success there, which was the main reason for their continuing there a long time.

Persecution and opposition often may be attended with singular success of the gospel. The UHC was formed within the African American struggle and rejection. The people endured persecution and opposition but still remained physically powerful and achieved immense success. It was a long and fruitful adventure, marked by the wondrous blend of physical sickness, pain, and rejection, that produced strong, growing churches and the greatest satisfaction any Christian in any age can know—that he or she has communicated the gospel.

The success the UHC obtained is described by Bishop Fisher, one of the early leaders of the UHC. He tells how a group of sharecroppers was able to build the largest sanctuary in the eastern part of North Carolina during a major depression in the United States. Bishop Fisher shared how the "believers would send monies in month after month and week after week until they were able to complete what was known as the Bible Training Institute."[27] This attitude of giving shows particular resemblance to the children of Israel after they completed their exodus from Egypt. Through UHC devotion and speaking boldly in the Lord and giving their personal testimonies about the grace and favor of God, God revealed great signs and wonders following this group of believers called the UHC.

Acts 14:3 also informs believers that the apostles were "speaking boldly in the Lord." The believers in the Bible spoke in the cause of the Lord Jesus, or in His name and by His authority. But perhaps, also, the expression includes the idea of their trusting in the Lord. Their continuous testimonies bore witness to the truth of their message, as miracles were worked through them. It is the Lord Jesus to whom reference is made, and this shows that, though bodily absent, He was still working miracles, still clothed with power, and still displaying that power in the advancement

---

27   Henry L. Fisher, *The History of the United Holy Church of America, Inc.* (Durham, NC: privately printed, 1945), 24.

of His cause. The conversion of sinners accomplished by Him is always a testimony, as proclaimed by cheering laborers and messages of His servants. One can see how that was beneficial for the saints of old in the UHC and how it can be beneficial today.

Spontaneous-style worship has been therapeutic for centuries in the black church as a whole, and not only in the UHC. However, embracing only the new contemporary-style worship without blending it with the old leaves people in the throes of suffering and oppression without the therapeutic means to get them through their pains and into the presence of God. This is an indispensable source in doing theology.

Communion/Fellowship

Communion and fellowship are major aspects of biblical worship. Many see worship as the coming together of a committed people, where believers seek direction, power, and inspiration as the chosen people of God, and UHC believers see the power of God revealed daily in the life of the UHC. The UHC celebrates Communion (Eucharist), not as a memorial but as a sacramental rite of the church, and most of the churches in the UHC carry out this celebration on a quarterly basis. When they take the sacrament of Holy Communion, it symbolizes their total rededication to personal participation in the struggle of black people and total rededication to the UHC. The devotional service highlights fellowship because it allows all to participate in the body of Christ.

There is a real embodiment of Christ's presence among African Americans. "This means that African-American Christians must recover the image of the Body of Christ as trope for their communal experience and the solidarity they seek. This emphasis upon unity in the body of Christ is essential for the black church's self-understanding."[28]

---

28   James H. Evans, Jr., *We Have Been Believers: An African-American Systematic Theology* (Minneapolis: Fortress, 1992), 131.

It is essential that worshipers are able to recognize the body for what it is— that they are all the body of Christ and must commune together to be that force that God intended the church to be. This is a major problem within the body of Christendom, because we have not truly learned how to discern the Lord's body, as Paul said. When believers gather and give space for everyone to share, they become conscious discerners of the body of Christ, because when worshipers assemble each person represents a part of Christ's body and is given a chance to contribute.

So as we practice the biblical principles of spontaneity during devotional services, we embody the concept of gathering together, which denotes communion or fellowship. Paul speaks of both communion and fellowship, using the same Greek term *koinonia*.[29] Paul uses this term to express the believers' relationship with the risen Lord and the benefits of salvation that come through Him. Paul used the "*koin*-stem" to describe the fellowship among the disciples in 1 Corinthians 10:16, stating, "The cup of blessing which we bless, is it not the communion of the blood of Christ? The bread which we break, is it not the communion of the body of Christ?" (KJV).

For Paul "the cup of blessing which we bless" is presented in this verse and the following verses as proof that Christians, by partaking of the Lord's Supper, are solemnly set apart to the service of the Lord Jesus; that they acknowledge Him as their Lord and dedicate themselves to Him; and that as they could not be devoted to idols and to the Lord Jesus at the same time, so they should not participate in the feasts in honor of idols or in the celebrations in which idolaters are engaged.

The expression "cup of blessing" evidently refers to the wine used in the celebration of the Lord's Supper. It is called "the cup of blessing" because when the cup is received the Christians praise or bless God for His mercy in providing redemption. It is not because it is the means of conveying a blessing to the souls

---

29   Donald K. McKim, *Westminster Dictionary of Theological Terms* (Louisville: Westminster John Knox, 1996), 154.

of those who partake of it—though that is true—but because thanksgiving, blessing, and praise for the benefits of redemption are rendered to God in the celebration.

Reading the Word

The reading of the Word of God brings redemption and liberates a life through the sharing of the Word of God. Another biblical principle, and a part of the devotional service, is the reading of Scripture, which is mentioned in the following verses.

> Blessed is he that readeth, and they that hear the words of this prophecy, and keep those things which are written therein: for the time is at hand. (Rev. 1:3)

> After the reading from the Law of Moses and from the writings of the prophets, the officials of the synagogue sent them a message: "Friends, we want you to speak to the people if you have a message of encouragement for them." (Acts 13:15)

> Until I come, give your time and effort to the public reading of the Scriptures and to preaching and teaching. (1 Tim. 4:13)

> -"Blessed is he that readeth" in Revelation 1:3 is regarded as a privilege extended with many blessings to those who mark the disclosures made in this book; that is, the important revelations respecting future times. Professor Stuart supposes that this refers to "those who listened to the public readers, and that both reader and hearer should regard themselves as highly favored."[30] Through

---

30   Gordon D. Fee and Douglas Stuart, *How to Read the Bible For All Its*

the devotional service, believers gain the favor of God from hearing the Word read in public.

Acts 13:15 supports the reading aloud of Scripture in devotional services and also encourages the members to share the Word with others. Wesley states,

> And after the reading of the law and the prophets, the chief of the synagogue sent to them - The law and it was read over once every year, a portion of it every Sabbath: to which was added a lesson taken out of the prophets. After this was over, any one might speak to the people, on any subject he thought convenient. Yet it was a circumstance of decency which Paul and Barnabas would hardly omit, to acquaint the rulers with their desire of doing it: probably by some message before the service began."[31]

Jesus Himself promoted and demonstrated the public reading of Scripture in Luke 4. He had returned to his hometown of Nazareth and while there, as custom dictated, He entered the synagogue on the Sabbath. He was handed the book of Isaiah, and He read, "The Spirit of the Lord is upon me" (Luke 4:18; cf. Isa. 61:1).

Reading Luke 4 and Acts 13:15 takes my mind immediately back to a Jewish bar mitzvah service I attended in Peabody, Massachusetts.[32] The rabbi called for those of the congregation to come and read the Scripture aloud to those in the synagogue. This rite was dressed in the fabric of devotional-style worship because the worship was not restricted to the pulpit but spread throughout the congregation. One person's participation represented the whole

---

Worth: A Guide to Understanding the Bible (Grand Rapids: Zondervan, 1993), 232-34

31 John Wesley, *Wesley's Explanatory Notes on the Whole Bible* (E-Sword computer program), on Acts 13:15.

32 Temple Ner Tamid of Peabody, Massachusetts, May 26, 2007

congregation. This celebration also represented the youth being prepared to participate in congregational worship, which mirrors the UHC devotional-style worship.

Devotional Singing

"Old Time Religion"[33]

I agree with the basic argument of Lincoln and Mamiya in their chapter called "The Performed Word: Music and the Black Church."[34] They give a persuasive explanation for the origin of what has become known as the traditional black church style of worship. The black church tradition of singing that was born during slavery was a new institution that never before existed.

33　*"Old Time Religion" by Ernest Watson. http://www.blackartdepot.com/ blackchurch.htm*

34　C, Eric Lincoln and Lawrence H. Mamiya, *The Black Church in the African American Experience* (Durham: Duke University Press, 2001), 346.

This new style of singing was born in the "invisible church"[35] as souls bellowed with spontaneous singing. The biblical principles for spontaneity during devotional services are the framework for coming together to sing psalms, hymns, and spiritual songs. Paul's words in Ephesians 5:19 furnish us a theological principle for this type of devotion. Paul stated in Ephesians 5:19, "Speak to one another with the words of psalms, hymns, and sacred songs; sing hymns and psalms to the Lord with praise in your hearts" (GNT).

The fifth chapter of Ephesians shows that the Spirit-filled, early church was a singing church. The dominant theme was joy. It was a thankful church, knowing who God was and what He had done and keeping at the surface of their awareness the fact that they were the recipients of unmerited mercy and grace. Gratitude was the keynote of their life. They saw themselves as all in the same boat, so they respected one another. Wesley says that "by there being no inspired songs, peculiarly adapted to the Christian dispensation, as there were to the Jewish, it is evident that the promise of the Holy Ghost to believers, in the last days, was by his larger effusion to supply the lack of it. Singing with your hearts - As well as your voice. To the Lord - Jesus, who searcheth the heart."[36] The Holy Spirit's promise to believers in the last days is to aid believers in singing with the heart and with the voice to the Lord. That is why Ephesians 5:19 covers so vividly areas that fit the black church tradition of devotional services. Ephesians 5:19 is unpacked as follows to fit the UHC tradition.

Speaking to yourselves: Speaking among yourselves is "endeavoring to edify one another and to promote purity of heart, by songs of praise. This has the force of a command, and it is a matter of obligation on Christians. From the beginning, praise was an important part of public worship, and is designed to be to the end of the world. . . . Nothing is more clear than that it

---

35 Lincoln and Mamiya, *The Black Church in the African American Experience,* 346.

36 Wesley, *Wesley's Explanatory Notes.*

was practiced by the Savior Himself and the apostles (see Mat. 26:30), and by the primitive church, as well as by the great body of Christians in all ages."[37]

In psalms: "The psalms of David were sung by the Jews at the temple, and by the early Christians."[38] Matthew 26:30 makes mention of hymns being sung at the close of Passover. "The singing of those psalms has constituted a delightful part of public worship in all ages. They speak the language of devotion at all times, and a large part of them are as well suited to the services of the sanctuary now as they were when first composed.[39] Fee and Stuart, in *Reading the Bible for All It's Worth,* open for us the psalms of lament to allow us to see the heart and pain of the psalmist. Worshipers need a place like a devotional-style service to release such pains in hymns.

And hymns. Albert Barnes notes,

> It is not easy to determine precisely what is the difference in the meaning of the words used here, or to designate the kind of compositions that were used in the early churches. A "hymn" is properly a song or ode in honor of God. Among the pagan it was a song in honor of some deity. With us now it denotes a short poem, composed for religious service, and sung in praise to God. Such brief poems were common among the pagan, and it was natural that Christians should early introduce and adopt them. Whether any of them were composed by the apostles it is impossible now to determine, though the presumption is very strong that if they had been they would have been preserved with as much care as their epistles, or as the Psalms. One thing is proved clearly by this passage, that there

---

37   Albert Barnes, *Barnes' Notes on the Bible* (E-Sword computer program), on Eph. 5:19.

38   Barnes, *Barnes' Notes on the Bible.*

39   Barnes, *Barnes' Notes on the Bible.*

were other compositions used in the praise of God
than the Psalms of David; and if it was right then
to make use of such compositions, it is now. They
were not merely "Psalms" that were sung, but
there were hymns and odes.[40]

Most hymns sung today in the UHC are hymns written by
Charles Wesley. "All of Wesley's hymns were written following
his conversion. Horrified by the mistreatment of slaves, which
he witnessed in Georgia (but not necessarily horrified by slavery
itself), Wesley petitioned God to allow the blood of Christ to free
our enslaved foreparents of their "curse" (stanzas one and three [of
the hymn "For the Heathens"]):

> Lord over all, if thou has made,
> Hast ransomed every soul of man,
> Why the grace is so long delayed,
> Why unfulfilled the saving plan?
> The bliss for Adam's race designed
> When will it reach to all mankind?
>
> The servile progeny of Ham
> Seize as the purchase of thy blood;
> Let all the heathens know thy name;
> From idols to the living God
> Their blinded votaries convert,
> And shine in every pagan heart.[41]

These hymns, such as the one above, were written from the
mind-set that blacks were the "cursed sons of Ham," and there
are other hymns written with the same view. So when we sing
the hymns of Wesley, we should be cognizant that we are singing
the hymns of one who believed that blacks were cursed and may

---

40   Barnes, *Barnes' Notes on the Bible.*
41   Jon Michael Spencer, *Sing a New Song: Liberating Black Hymnody*
(Minneapolis: Fortress, 1995), 120-21.

still have been thinking that way at his death. This is not to say Wesley's songs should not be used in worship, because Charles Wesley wrote over "6500 hymns covering all the festivals of the Christian faith."[42] They include songs such as, "A Charge to Keep I Have," "Hark, the Herald Angels Sing," "Jesus Christ is Risen Today," and many more; however, we all need to be selective and remain true to each individual's culture of worship.[43]

Spiritual songs: Spiritual songs also are considered to be "odes." According to Barnes, odes are songs

relating to spiritual things in contradistinction from these which were sung in places of festivity and revelry. An "ode" is properly a short poem or song adapted to be set to music, or to be sung; a lyric poem. In what way these were sung in New Testament times, it is now vain to conjecture. Whether with or without instrumental accompaniments; whether by a choir or by the assembly; whether by an individual only, or whether they were by responses, it is not possible to decide from anything in the New Testament. It is probable that it would be done in the simplest manner possible. Yet as music constituted so important a part of the worship of the temple, it is evident that the early Christians would be by no means indifferent to the nature of the music which they had in their churches. And as it was so important a part of the worship of the pagan gods, and contributed so much to maintain the influence of paganism, it is not unlikely that the early Christians would feel the importance of making their music attractive, and of making it tributary to the support of religion. If there is attractive music at the banquet, and in the theater, contributing to the maintenance of amusements where God is forgotten, assuredly the music of the sanctuary should not be such as to disgust those of pure and refined taste.[44]

The spirituals in the black church are expressed in the full range of emotion and life experience of the slave—negative and

---

42   Spencer, *Sing a New Song*, 121.
43   Spencer, *Sing a New Song*, 121.
44   Barnes, *Barnes' Notes on the Bible*.

positive. W. E. B. Du Bois called them "Sorrow Songs."[45] The spiritual was considered to be "the music of an unhappy people, of the children of disappointment."[46] Maynard-Reid talks about the spiritual within the black church: "African American slave forefathers and mothers not only borrowed and transformed existing hymns but created new songs and invented new tunes. The date of origin of the spiritual as a musical genre cannot be determined with precision, but it apparently emerged on Southern plantations during the antebellum slave period and evolved as a musical form in the 'praise houses' of the South and independent black churches of the North."[47] These songs lend themselves well to the Spirit-filled devotional services, where the Spirit is seen to spontaneously lead the service to create new determination to ascend to the place in God.

Singing: "The prevailing character of music in the worship of God should be vocal. If instruments are employed, they should be so subordinate that the service may be characterized as singing."[48] Within the black church the preaching is the focal point of worship, and all other activities find their place in some subsidiary relationship. In the UIIC music, or more precisely singing, is second only to preaching as the attraction and the primary vehicle of spiritual transport for the worshiping congregation. Lincoln and Mamiya state, "Good preaching and singing are almost invariably the minimum conditions of a successful ministry. Both activities trace their roots back to Africa where music and religion and life itself were all one holistic enterprise."[49] It is often stated that in the black church, and even in the Southern District Convocation

---

45   W. E. B. Du Bois, *The Souls of Black Folk* (New York: Fawcett, 1961), 186.

46   Du Bois, *The Souls of Black Folk,* 179.

47   Pedrito U. Maynard-Reid, *Diverse Worship: African-American, Caribbean & Hispanic Perspectives* (Downers Grove, IL: InterVarsity, 2000), 76-77.

48   Barnes, *Barnes' Notes on the Bible.*

49   Lincoln and Mamiya, *The Black Church in the African American Experience,* 346.

(SDC), an affiliate of UHC, songs are sung in a kind of ritualistic cadence that bleeds down to the prayers and sermons in the black church.

And making melody: Once again, Albert Barnes explains the meaning:

> "Melody" is an agreeable succession of sounds; a succession so regulated and modulated as to please the ear. It differs from "harmony," inasmuch as melody is an agreeable succession of sounds by a single voice; harmony consists in the accordance of different sounds. It is not certain, however, that the apostle here had reference to what is properly called "melody." The word which he uses . . . means to touch, twitch, pluck—as the hair, the beard; and then to twitch a string—to "twang" it—as the string of a bow, and then the string of an instrument of music. It is most frequently used in the sense of touching or playing a lyre, or a harp; and then it denotes to make music in general, to sing—perhaps usually with the idea of being accompanied with a lyre or harp. It is used, in the New Testament, only in Rom 5:19; 1Co 14:15, where it is translated "sing;" in Jam 5:13, where it is rendered "sing psalms," and in the place before us. The idea here is, that of singing in the heart, or praising God from the heart. The psalms, and hymns, and songs were to be sung so that the heart should be engaged, and not so as to be mere music, or a mere external performance.[50]

To the Lord: This phrase refers to praise of the Lord or praise that is addressed to the Lord.

---

50   Barnes, *Barnes' Notes on the Bible.*

Singing, as here meant, is a direct and solemn act of worship, and should be considered such as really as prayer. In singing we should regard ourselves as speaking directly to God, and the words, therefore, should be spoken with a solemnity and awe becoming such a direct address to the great Yahweh. So Pliny says of the early Christians, "Carmenquc Christo quasi Deo dicere secure invicem" - "and they sang among themselves hymns to Christ as God." If this be the true nature and design of public psalmody, then it follows:

1. That all should regard it as an act of solemn worship in which they should engage—in "heart" at least, if they cannot themselves sing.

2. Public psalmody should not be entrusted wholly to the light and frivolous; to the trifling and careless part of a congregation.

3. They who conduct this part of public worship ought to be pious. The leader "ought" to be a Christian; and they who join in it "ought" also to give their hearts to the Redeemer. Perhaps it would not be proper to say absolutely that no one who is not a professor of religion should take part in the exercises of a choir in a church; but there can be no error in saying that such persons "ought" to give themselves to Christ, and to sing from the heart. Their voices would be nonetheless sweet; their music no less pure and beautiful; nor could their own pleasure in the service be lessened. A choir of sweet singers in a church - united in the same praises here—"ought" to be prepared to join in the same, praises around the throne of God.[51]

---

51   Barnes, *Barnes' Notes on the Bible.*

This shows us that not only the United Holy Church but also all worshipers need to make sure that worship features whole-person participation of the whole community. The issue arises as one of "imaging" the Tri-unity of God through congregational participation in our worship.[52] Worship is intended to be a participatory act of the people of God. This was plainly the case with Old Testament worship.[53] In the New Testament, as well, everyone was to bring something to the gathering for the good of the whole (1 Cor. 14:26). As seen earlier, Paul wrote also of the importance of the congregation's ministry to one another in singing and teaching (Col. 3:16; Eph. 5:19-20). Paul also mentioned the exercise of the various spiritual gifts in 1 Corinthians 12 and 14, as well as in Romans 12. And the people are to respond to what is shared through these various gifts and to what they have heard in the services by saying "the Amen" (1 Cor. 14:16; 2 Cor. 1:20).

Too often worship services in our churches reduce the vast majority of participants to passive observers rather than active participants. Our aim should be that the whole assembly is actively engaged in the worship of God and that they are encouraged to bless the LORD with all that is within them (Ps. 103:1)—heart, soul, mind, and strength (Mark 12:29-31). God is worthy of all that we have, and nothing should be held back. It is the whole person who needs to be transformed into the likeness of Christ. Dallas Willard calls this type of transformation "renovation of the heart."[54] He states that this takes place when we absorb our minds and hearts in worship; then spiritual transformation takes place. Believers must offer the Lord the raw materials of our cognition and affections. Our thinking, our will, and our emotions are all fallen and in need of being more wholly reconciled to God. Scripture allows us to remember, the believers in Corinth whom Paul urged to "be reconciled to God" (2 Cor. 5:20). Because we

---

52   Palmer, *Art of Conducting Public Worship*, 197.
53   Palmer, *Art of Conducting Public Worship*, 198.
54   Dallas Willard, *Renovation of the Heart: Putting on the Character of Christ* (Colorado Springs: NavPress, 2002), 17.

are not yet living fully for the one who died for us and rose again (2 Cor. 5:15), we place all that is within us before the Lord and ask Him to change us further into His likeness as we worship Him.

Our bodies, too, are called into action. Our ears hear, our eyes watch, and our lips speak, sing, shout, and close. We lift our hands and clap our hands. We bend our knees to kneel and straighten them to stand. We greet one another with our voices, our eyes, and with a handshake, hug, or holy kiss. Those who design worship gatherings for the congregation must keep the whole community in mind as they do so. And as they think of the individuals in that community, they must think of whole persons. The traditional aspects of worship within the UHC summon the total man holistically.

Praise and Worship

Praise and worship seems to be universal. Has anyone ever heard of an explorer finding a new tribe or culture that doesn't worship? I'm of the opinion that worship is a natural instinct and a basic need of every person. Worship is central to every church congregation, because it expresses and shapes congregational life. Worship also must be seen as a principal avenue for the nurture and maintenance of a congregation's spiritual life, because what happens in worship greatly impacts the quality of people's faith and commitment. A simple definition of worship is to regard with great devotion or to honor as a divine being. Take a second to think about what you are most devoted to in this life, and ask yourself, "Is it worthy of my devotion; do I worship a divine being?"[55]

Kathy Black shares how "throughout the years people have tried to articulate worship and what worship does."[56] People do not all worship the same God, but everyone worships something

---

55 Kathy Black, *Culturally Conscious Worship* (St. Louis: Chalice, 2000), 81.

56 Black, *Culturally Conscious Worship*, 83-84.

or someone. Since all worship, all should question the reason for this desire. The most logical conclusion is that people were created by a higher being for the very purpose of worship.

The ongoing quest of man is to find answers to the fundamental questions of human origin, human nature, and human destiny. There is one book that has the answers to all these questions, including questions about worship. The Bible is the wonderful and mysterious book that God has chosen as a way to communicate with humanity.

God is the focus of devotion in both the Old and New Testaments. In Exodus 20:2-3, God says, "I am the LORD your God . . . You shall have no other gods before me." And in Matthew 4:10, Jesus says, "Worship the Lord your God and serve him only." Worship, then, is not merely a natural instinct; it is a command from God.

The contemporary movement of praise and worship holds that God alone is worthy of our devotion, praise, and worship. He is God, the Creator, and people are commanded to praise and worship Him. I am of the opinion that the traditional, devotional-style worship holds to the same concept.

Psalm 96:9 says, "Worship the Lord in the splendor of his holiness; tremble before him, all the earth." Psalm 29:2 says, "Give unto the Lord the glory due his name; worship the Lord in the beauty of holiness." Robert Webber stresses that "worship is a verb,"[57] mainly because worship is service. Peterson states, "According to the book Exodus, Israel's redemption from slavery [a major correlation to the black church] was to release the people for service [a verb form of worship] to God on the mountain where he first revealed himself to Moses (Ex. 3:12)."[58] Serving the Lord is a comprehensive term, and "without worship, we go about

---

57   Robert E. Webber, *Worship Is a Verb: Eight Principles for Transforming Worship* (Peabody, MA: Hendrickson, 1995), 2.

58   David Peterson, *Engaging With God: A Biblical Theology of Worship* (Downers Grove, IL: InterVarsity, 1992), 65.

miserable."[59] God doesn't want His people to be miserable—He has a perfect plan for our lives. He has done many things to show us that He loves us and does not want us to be miserable. He wants us to have hope for a future with Him—He wants us to have eternal life in heaven with Him.

A life of praise and worship fills our deepest needs, and, amazingly, it also brings great joy to God. Zephaniah 3:17 states, "The LORD your God is with you, he is mighty to save. He will take great delight in you, he will quiet you with his love, he will rejoice over you with singing."

God tells people how to praise and worship him in His Word. John 4:23 says, "Yet a time is coming and has now come when the true worshipers will worship the Father in spirit and truth, for they are the kind of worshipers the Father seeks" (NIV). In order to worship God in truth, we need to know that Jesus said, "I am the way and the truth and the life. No one comes to the Father except through me." So, before one can worship in the way that God desires, one has to develop a relationship with Him through faith in Jesus, His Son. Marcina Wiederkehr says that our problem is that we have "gotten used to the cheap grace of being uninvolved. We've gotten used to worshiping with hearts that aren't converted. Worship coming from an unconverted heart can only be empty ritual."[60] The real need for renewal of worship is the renewal of hearts, making them receptive to the movement of God's Spirit. The best way we can praise and worship God is with our every thought and action. Romans 12:1-2 states, "Therefore, I urge you, brothers, in view of God's mercy, to offer your bodies as living sacrifices, holy and pleasing to God—this is your spiritual act of worship. Do not conform any longer to the pattern of this world, but be transformed by the renewing of your mind. Then you will be able to test and approve what God's will is—his good, pleasing, and perfect will."

---

59   Peterson, *Engaging With God,* 66.

60   Wiederkehr, Macrina, A *Tree Full of Angels: Seeing the Holy in the Ordinary.*(San Francisco: HarperSan Francisco, 1988), pg. 23

Traditional, devotional-style worship and contemporary praise and worship are drinking from the same fountain. The problem is that people are so busy drinking from their own view that they cannot take the time to grasp what the other style is doing. The praise and worship group seeks to make a case for the progression from praise to worship on the basis of the Psalms. Indeed, in Psalm 95, "praise" happens to be mentioned in verse 2 and "worship" in verse 6; therefore, praise comes before worship. However, in Psalm 66 praise and worship are used interchangeably, and there's no neat separation between God's being, deeds, and name. The distinctions are artificial, and there is no support for them in the psalms. Also, the notion that praising God for what He is represents a higher expression than thanking God for what He does is foreign to the Psalms.

Also, the idea in praise and worship is that worship is to be dominated by praise, because the Psalms show us this pattern. However, the Psalms also are taken up with lament and appeals to God to help His people. To imply that petition and lament are an inferior mode of communication with God does injustice to the Psalms and ignores a major teaching of Scripture—that God takes our sin seriously, and all are earthen vessels in need of a holy God.

As people enter the presence of a holy God, they come to a Father who loves, forgives, and adopts them by grace into His family and invites them to be seated as honored guests at His table. Carol Doran and Thomas H. Troeger share their concern in a book entitled *Trouble at the Table: Gathering the Tribes for Worship.*[61] We find out that God has invited people to the table where He provides everything they need, and He has placed them at the table where they feel most comfortable because they are with their own tribe. Doran and Troeger, however, mention the problem of "'tribes' asserting themselves in ways that entangled,

---

61   Carol Doran and Thomas H. Troeger, *Trouble at the Table: Gathering the Tribes for Worship* (Nashville: Abingdon, 1992), 11.

strained, and sometimes broke the community apart."[62] That is why the church group called UHC must analyze the causes so that their future can be more effective.

It is the hope of this work that the effectiveness in UHC and black church worship will be seen in worship filling their prayers, songs, creeds, offerings, and sacraments in devotional-style worship and praise and worship; in the re-presentation of the gospel for justification and sanctification in multiple ways throughout the corporate worship; in musical expressions that carry biblically sound content in songs that express heartfelt worship as dialogue between God and His people; and in worship that is amazed over and over again at the grace of God for undeserving sinners, appropriated and applied to lives by the Holy Spirit, whether in the traditional-style worship service or the praise-and-worship-style service, because we are worship reformers and heirs of King David. "It was King David who focused their common interests. He brought them [the tribes of Israel] together by the power of his charisma and by moving the ark of the covenant, the most sacred symbol of their worship, to Jerusalem."[63] The ark is a symbol of the Godhead, or the Trinity, who desires to bring the UHC together because they are heirs. They are also part of a religious experience that brought people together to form Christian institutions prior to the emancipation. This is an experience our next chapter will discuss further.

---

62   Doran and Troeger, *Trouble at the Table*, 13-14.
63   Doran and Troeger, *Trouble at the Table*, 15.

CHAPTER 3

LITERATURE REVIEW
"Blessed are those who have learned to acclaim you"
Psalm 89:15

"The religious experience of the majority of blacks who were involved in Christian institutions before emancipation was so closely intertwined with their total life experience that the starting point in understanding the meaning of that religious life must be the total life experience."[64] According to Payne, slaves represent the earliest group of African Americans to ever form a religious organization. Enslaved Africans who were transported to the New World, beginning in the fifteenth century, brought with them a wide range of local religious beliefs and practices. From these newly settled people in America, churches arose that shared similar focus to that of the United Holy Church. These churches included the African Baptist Church, Free African Society, African American Episcopal Congregation, African Zoar Methodist, Bethel A.M.E Church, Colored Primitive Baptists of America, United Free Will Baptist Denominations, Reformed Zion Union Apostolic Churches, Church of Christ Holiness, Church of God, Church of God in Christ, Church of God Sanctified Church, and Fire Baptized Holiness Church of the

---

64   Wardell J. Payne, ed., *Directory of African American Religious Bodies,* 2nd ed. (Washington, DC: Howard University Press, 1995), 3.

Americas. The majority of these churches were birthed through the Holiness Movement. According to Payne, a contributor of the Holiness Movement stated, "There are so many exciting subjects constantly brought before the American public that churches cannot command attention without very exciting preaching to get the public ear."[65]

Churches that supported these revivals were called "free churches." Many Baptists, most Methodists, Churches of Christ, and later Bible churches, all stand in this tradition. Some of these groups brought their simple forms of worship from Europe but revised them during the nineteenth century. That modified pattern, still used in many traditional, non-liturgical churches today, reflected a passion to evangelize the unconverted. The freest churches of all were the black congregations formed during slavery. Gospel and soul music was born in the rhythmic worship of African American churches, where every worship service was an emancipation proclamation.

> He set me free, He set me free.
> He broke the chains of bondage for me.
> I'm glory bound, my Jesus to see.
> Glory to God. He set me free![66]

This free or frontier style of worship, whether white or black, usually began with a "song service" (i.e., devotional-style worship) to elevate the emotional pitch of the congregation. Impromptu prayers added an intensely personal note. After an offering was received "for the spread of the gospel," a choir sang a gospel song emphasizing conversion or personal holiness.[67] Then the service reached its climax with an evangelistic sermon and an "altar call" to the unconverted or unsanctified. And many came.

---

65   Payne, ed., *Directory of African American Religious Bodies,* 5.
66   Verolga Nix *Songs of Zion* (Nashville: Abingdon Press, 1981), 45
67   Pedrito U. Maynard-Reid, *Diverse Worship: African-American, Caribbean & Hispanic Perspectives* (Downers Grove, IL: InterVarsity, 2000), 72.

Worship then, as today in seeker-sensitive churches, primarily served evangelistic purposes.

The literature review in this chapter will deal with the Methodist black church in America, from which the United Holy Church founders were banned, and their practice of the same type of devotional services. Also, we will explore the Brethren Church, which is a mostly Caucasian church born out of the Anabaptist movement during the Reformation. We will also look at the Fire Baptized Assembly of God denomination, which is also similar to the United Holy Church in their beliefs and devotional practices. First Presbyterian and Valley Baptist Church are individual churches that also present a fiber of familiarity to the United Holy Church.

Despite the diversity of ways we flesh out worship in actual ritual performance from denomination to denomination, from church to church, and from culture to culture, there is some unity in what we do. The two methods of worship found within the United Holy Church are under consideration in this thesis. One offers worship that is said to be contemporary in flavor; the other has a more traditional style.

Christian worship opens us to several experiences in worship to help form community. The great thing about Christianity is that God allows us all to worship Him from our own cultural experiences. Robert Webber lists several areas of worship that help us to grasp the freedom given through our experiences. Webber speaks of the contemporary praise and worship renewal in the Holiness-Pentecostal worship, liturgical reform in the Roman Catholic Church, and worship renewal among mainline Protestant Churches all because of the praise and worship movement.[68]

A portion of the United Holy Church holds to devotional service, which is a black church style of worship that the author experienced in the Church of God in Christ and the black Baptist church. Devotion simply means giving one's best, whether one

---

68   Robert E. Webber, *Worship Old & New: A Biblical Historical, and Practical Introduction* (Grand Rapids: Zondervan, 1984),126-32.

is a golden-throated choir member, a tone-deaf congregant, or somewhere in between. Primarily, devotional service means active and simultaneous participation by parents, elders, youths, and children, not standing with arms folded, looking at the ceiling, or worrying about the color of someone's dress, or the pot roast in the oven, or rifling through a box of crayons in a children's worship packet. It means focused attention to words and music, whether people consider themselves singers or not. It means anticipating the presence of God's Word in the hymn or anthem—and actively listening for it. Devotion means to participate the best one can, giving God the best always.

Toward a Definition of Worship

This literature review will note various ways in which Christian thinkers speak about worship. Worship has innumerable forms. The Muslims worship Allah in prayer by turning toward Mecca five times a day and repeating the same prayer. At some time in a Muslim's life he makes a pilgrimage to Mecca, where he will walk around the Kaaba seven times and kiss the sacred black stone. An American Indian may have worshiped by erecting a totem pole, offering up tobacco in the peace pipe, or by sacrificing a finger joint or even a human being. Satan worshipers allegedly sacrifice infants and use some of the organs of mutilated animals. Christians see these forms of worship as misguided and erroneous, although those who follow these practices do so with great sincerity.

Then, of course, there are the pagan forms of worship we find within civilized America. There are those who worship the sun by taking off their clothes in nudist colonies. There are those who would have us understand that they find it much easier to worship God on the golf course or in front of the television watching football on Sunday.

The Importance of Worship

Some may wonder why all the fuss over this matter of worship. Before we try to define what worship is, let's first deal with the importance of worship. The first reason for our study of worship has already been suggested. Simply stated, believers need to study worship because there is so much confusion and so little understanding and practice of worship.

Negatively, there is a second reason we should search the Scriptures on the subject of worship. It is because of the severe consequences of false worship. God rejected Cain's sacrifice because it was false worship (Gen. 4:5). Three thousand people died in one day because of the false worship of the golden calf fashioned by Aaron (Exodus 32). The kingdom of Israel was divided because of the idolatry and false worship of the nation (1 Kings 11:31-33). The fall of Jerusalem was directly attributable to the apostasy and false worship of the nation (Jer. 1:16; 16:11; 22:9). Misdirected worship was the cause of untold hardship and suffering in the Old Testament. In the first chapter of Romans, Paul wrote that God was justified in condemning man because he worshiped in error: "For they exchanged the truth of God for a lie, and worshiped and served the creature rather than the Creator, who is blessed forever. Amen" (v. 25). Satan fell from heaven because he sought worship for himself rather than submit to his Creator. Satan today seeks those who will worship and serve him (Matt. 4:9).

The third reason, and by far the primary one for considering the subject of worship worthy of our consideration, is because worship is of great importance to God. That is the clear teaching of passages such as John 4: "But an hour is coming, and now is, when the true worshipers shall worship the Father in spirit and truth; for such people the Father seeks to be His worshipers" (John 4:23). God is seeking men and women to be worshipers of Him. But this worship must be worship that is "in spirit and in truth." It is not enough to be a worshiper of God; God is seeking true worshipers. It is only in the Word of God that we can learn what worship is pleasing to God.

Why, then, should people devote themselves to the study of worship? Christians must do so simply because it is a matter of great importance to God and because false worship has dire consequences. With all the current confusion on the subject, Christians must return to the Scriptures for our infallible guide to true worship that pleases God.

Words Used for Worship

James White, professor of Christian worship at Perkins School of Theology, Southern Methodist University, discusses Peter Brunner's term Gottesdienst.

> The German "Gottesdienst" means "service to God," but the tricky question is whether to take the genitive, "Gottes-," "God's service, " as an objective or subjective genitive. The former would make God the object of the action in serving; Gottesdienst in this sense would be "serving God" and implies much of what "worship" does—honor, veneration, acts of homage, e.g. in cult. The subjective genitive, however, takes the "Gottes-" part of the compound as the subject of the action serving, and so the sense is "God's serving us." Worship, on that reading, means when God ministers to [us] and brings the Good News and…grace into [our] lives.[69]

The latter definition of the term means, "God doing something for believers which they cannot do for themselves." The German scholar Ferdinand Hahn understands the term in just this sense:

---

69   James F. White, *Introduction to Christian Worship* (Nashville: Abingdon, 1982), 23.

The basis of worship is God's saving action; word and sacraments are God's service to the community. Coupled with it is, however, also a reciprocal aspect, the response side from [human beings], namely service by the community before God. But as Professor reads the New Testament— and again this is characteristic of Evangelical thought, in light of Romans 12—the church's service before God takes place in the world and especially takes the form of service to the [sister or] brother.[70]

It appears that Hahn's term or point of view provides dualities, the first being God's service to human beings and the second human beings' service to God. The latter is seen not only as public religious ritual but as social action as well. Worship is both religious ritual and social action.

Frank Senn discusses the Greek term *leitourgia,* from which the word *liturgy* is derived.

Leitourgia derives from leition, "pertaining to the people," and ergon, meaning "work" or "service." The term is used variously in the New Testament to refer to the priestly service of Zechariah in the Temple (Luke 1:23), the sacrificial ministry of Christ (Heb. 8:6), the worship of the church (Acts 13:2), and the collecting of money for the poor and suffering saints (2 Cor. 9:12). In these New Testament uses of leitourgia the public and social dimensions of cult are exemplified. In its specific Christian use, liturgy is not only public worship but also social action.[71]

---

70 White, *Introduction to Christian Worship*, 24.
71 Frank Senn, *Christian Worship and Its Cultural Setting* (Philadelphia: Fortress, 1983), 6.

A brief glance at a good Bible concordance will reveal that there are a number of Greek and Hebrew words that are rendered "to worship" or "worshiper." In the Scriptures, there are three pairs of words that underscore for us the three primary elements of true worship.

Humility: The most frequent words related to worship in both the Old and New Testaments mean to make obeisance, to bow down, to prostrate. The Hebrew word is *shaha,* and the Greek word is *proskuneo.*[72] Both words denote the act of bowing or prostrating oneself in submissiveness and reverence. The outward posture reflects an inner attitude of humility and respect. The word might be used of men showing respect for men, as well as describing a response to deity. As the word relates to worship, it denotes a high view of God and a condescending opinion of self. Thus, true worship views God in His perfection and man in his imperfection.

Reverence: Another pair of terms underscores the attitude of reverence. The Hebrew word is *yare,* and the Greek term is *sebomai.*[73] The idea of both the Greek and the Hebrew is that of fearing God. It is not so much the fear of terror and dread so much as it is the fear of wonder and awe at the majesty and greatness of the infinite God; and Senn differentiates "humility" from "reverence"[74] in that the first pair of terms has an inward focus. We are aware of our finiteness and sinfulness in the light of His infinity and perfection. The second pair of terms focuses outwardly upon the awesome majesty of God. Irreverence is antithetical to worship. No doubt, it was the irreverence of the Corinthians at the Lord's Table that required such severe discipline as sickness and death (1 Cor. 11:30). Paul said that they did not "judge the body rightly" (1 Cor. 11:29). It seems Paul is saying that to participate in the Lord's Table, to partake of the elements that symbolize the

---

72   Franklin M. Segler. *Understanding, Preparing for, and Practicing Christian Worship* (Nashville: Broadman & Holman), 6-7.
73   Segler. *Understanding, Preparing for, and Practicing Christian Worship,* 7.
74   Senn, *Christian Worship and Its Cultural Setting,* 6.

body of our Lord, in a light or irreverent way is to bring upon us the discipline of God. Also, to improperly discern the body of Christ in the Lord's Table can bring sickness and death upon one's life. Drunkenness and frivolity at the Lord's Table reveals a spirit of irreverence that is diametrically opposed to true worship. The sacrament offers a foretaste of God's future reign when people will gather from the four corners of the earth to sit together at table.

Service: The third pair of terms employed for worship in the Bible emphasizes service. The Hebrew term *abad* and its Greek counterpart *latreuo* denote the idea "to work, to labor, or to serve."[75] In the Old Testament this service was most often priestly service. In the New Testament we are told that we are all priests of God (1 Peter 2:5, 9), so that this term does not apply only to the service of the few but to the entire congregation of believers in Christ.

In addition, service and worship were often linked in the Old Testament. It is no surprise, then, when we find Satan tempting our Lord to worship him (Luke 4:7). Satan was not asking our Lord simply to fall to the ground before him. He was asking the Lord to acknowledge him as sovereign and to surrender to him in service. This is why our Lord responded, "It is written, 'You shall worship the Lord your God and serve Him only'" (Luke 4:8). Worship and service cannot be isolated; rather they must be integrated, if there is to be true worship.

The Birthing of UHC

The United Holy Church came into being during a period of tremendous change. The late nineteenth century was a time of unrest that is perhaps unmatched in the history of the United States. The date given for the initial meeting from which the United Holy Church emerged is 1886. This is a little more than twenty years removed from the Civil War.

---

75   Segler. *Understanding, Preparing for, and Practicing Christian Worship,* 7.

During these days of the conception of our church, the nation was reckoning as never before with the presence of black men and women. In the eyes of the American population as a whole, the black presence was nothing more than a nuisance. Not many years before, prior to the Civil War, black people were slaves, hewers of wood, and drawers of water. We were counted along with mules and pigs as property of the slave owner.

Black women along with female livestock were for the purpose of breeding and reproducing more resources for sweat and labor. Even in those sections of the nation that abolished slavery before the war, black men and women were unwelcome. Their presence agitated the immigrants, who saw them as an impediment to the promise and dream America represented to them, and there was ever the threat of rioting and violence.

Battle of the Church

The church too was caught in a storm, as the United States was undergoing the pain of transition from a country and agrarian past to a modern, industrial, and urban era. No longer could farmers, entrepreneurs, and industrialists be left alone to earn according to their personal aggressiveness and ingenuity on the backs of slaves. Prior to the Civil War, there was hardly a question regarding the status of slaves and the absolute authority of their masters over them. But despite the generally inhumane treatment they received, slaves remained necessary to the economy.

The church had to wrestle with her mandate from the gospel as it related to the African who was brought to the shores of America as a slave. The black church that had been more or less unified in its purpose during the days of slavery could not remain remote. Before the war, all persons of African descent were either slaves or a step or two removed from slavery. Even in "freedom" and in "free" states, black people were subject to having their rights summarily stripped from them.

John Wesley - The Holiness View

The black church was following or gravitating to John Wesley and the holiness view. The Greek word for "holy" *(hagios)* means "sanctified," or set apart. Sanctified Christians came to believe that slavery was a blot on society and the church and that it should be abolished. Antislavery thought was the direct cause of the formation of the Wesleyan Methodist Church in New York and New England in 1843-44. The issue of slavery was ripping the Methodist Church from pillar to post. The debate ensued for some years and produced the following points.

> Methodist Episcopal Church having no rule forbidding slave-holding by private members; and by declaring that slave-holding is in harmony with the Golden rule, and by allowing Annual conferences to say that it is not a moral wrong, makes itself responsible for slavery:

> The government of the church is aristocratic (upper-class, noble) and its attitude toward dissenting (nonconformist rebellious) brethren is uncharitable.[76]

The fight continued until a split occurred over an article on sanctification that was prepared and inserted into the Discipline.

> Sanctification is that renewal of our fallen nature by the Holy Ghost, received through faith in Jesus Christ, whose blood of atonement cleanseth from all sin; whereby we are not only delivered form the guilt of sin, but are washed from its pollution,

---

76   Gayraud S. Wilmore, *Black Religion and Black Radicalism: An Interpretation of the Religious History of African Americans* (Maryknoll, NY: Orbis, 1998), 108

saved from its power, and are enabled, through grace, to love God with all our hearts, and to walk in His holy commandments blameless.[77]

This resulted in the birth of the "New Methodism," conservatives who were also called "Preachers-come-back-to-the-Disciple-Society."[78] B. T. Roberts was the leader, and he called for a free church where the work of holiness could be promoted. The points forming the basis for the separate organization were: doctrines and usage of primitive methods, such as the witness of the Spirit and entire sanctification as a state of grace distinct from justification and attainable instantaneously by faith; free seats and congregational singing, without instrumental music in all cases; plainness of dress, and an equal representation of ministers and layman in all councils of the church; no slaveholding, and no connection with oath-bound societies.

Now all this infighting did not escape the black church. In fact, it was due in large measure to her refusal to be passive that the storm did not fade away with easy victory to the forces of oppression based in religion devoid of holiness and prophetic social consciousness. From its inception, the black church was characterized by a religion that joyfully celebrated the Spirit's presence and an intense passion for freedom. Born as it was in the bowels of slavery, its life was stamped indelibly by marks of suffering and oppression. But those whose faith was in the God who brought the children of Israel out of Egypt and who is the Father of the Lord Jesus never doubted His love for them. Neither did they waver in their earnest expectation of the Holy Spirit, who was given as their comforter and guide.

The understanding of God that guided the mothers and fathers of the black church in the north prompted them to articulate clearly and forcefully their belief that God was on their side and that He would surely judge those who oppressed them. It was this

---

77 Wilmore, *Black Religion and Black Radicalism,* 201.
78 Wilmore, *Black Religion and Black Radicalism,* 202.

conviction that led Bishop Richard Allen, the patriarch of African Methodism, and those who followed him from Saint George's Church in refusing to suffer the humiliation of being snatched from their knees in prayer because of their color.

The slave preachers were powerful persons on the plantation. When the slaves did steal away to hold their meetings, their preachers informed them of a gracious God. So great was the power they developed within the slave community that these preachers came to be both hated and feared by slave owners. The preacher was considered to be the mouthpiece of God. The slave preacher was seen as an authority figure within the community. He was seen as having the answer to political concerns, marriage problems, and any other issue within the community.

It was in the south under the auspices of the "invisible institution"[79] that the enthusiastic, exciting traits of black religion were most pronounced. These secret meetings, outlawed in most states, were sometimes held early in the morning or at midnight. The way slaves worshiped nearly defied description. There was heartfelt singing that drew the entire body into the motion established by its rhythm. Accompanied by clapping hands and tossing of heads, such singing would continue for hours. When praise meetings were held in the woods near the swamps, pots were filled with water and placed around the perimeter, with their mouths turned toward the center of the gathering, to prevent the sound of the preaching and singing from carrying to the keen ears of paranoid masters and overseers.

Slave preaching also was filled with this rhythm and vibrancy. Most slaves endured the discourses of those preachers selected or permitted by their masters, but they made no secret of their preference to hear their own.

---

79   Wilmore, *Black Religion and Black Radicalism*, 25.

Separation of UHC: A Black Church

At the same time that Holiness associations were proliferating throughout the country and the black church was seeking an appropriate character for the new day, the Holiness Movement was beginning to spread to the south. According to Henry L. Fisher in his history of the United Holy Church of America, Inc., "The first meeting under the sponsorship of persons professing Holiness was held in a cottage in the town of Method, North Carolina, a suburb of Raleigh, the capital. The meeting was held on the first Sunday in May 1886, and in its wake the adherents to Holiness in the south rose into a great host."[80]

Worship Tradition of UHC

Much of the worship time was spent in prayer, which was the supreme sign that those present considered themselves in need. Prayer was accompanied by an expectation of manifestations, which would leave no doubt in the minds of any that the deity was present. Prayers were rarely rehearsed, for written prayers were thought not to be motivated by the Spirit.

Other acts of worship fell into the category of praise, which was a crucial ingredient in making and keeping the service what it was. It was the deep and abiding belief of the "holy people" that giving praise to God was their duty. Taking the words pertaining to praise from the Psalms as a definite command, they believed they were transgressing the will of God if they did not make a "joyful noise," that is, give praise with a loud noise, with clapping of hands, the loud-sounding instruments, the dance, and any other mode of expression that was available to them.

Praise was as much a part of the service as the reading of the Scriptures and preaching. Indeed, for "holy people" praise was

---

80   H. L. Fisher, *History of United Holy Church of America, Inc.* (Durham, NC: privately printed, 1945), 23.

much like a sacramental act: voluminous praise was interpreted as a sign that God's favor was on the meeting. During the meeting, persons acting as "praise leaders" were expected to lead devotional services. But in spontaneous moments, persons bringing greetings, presiding, introducing the speaker, or acting in some other formal capacity would sing praise songs or ask for some form of collective witness such as "lifting the hands if they were saved" or giving the Lord a "wave offering."[81]

Collective praise usually yielded tumultuous outbursts extending to lengthy moments in which the whole service would be enraptured. The metaphor used to describe the most tumultuous praise was that of "falling fire." In the falling of the fire, people would shout at the top of their voices, weep, dance, and speak with unknown tongues.

The praise that went forth in the services was full of zeal and vitality. As a matter of principle and commitment, "holy people" believed that they should make their deepest feelings known to one another and to the world, for what God had done on their behalf was no secret. This sort of expression became the trademark for "holy people." Praise was not merely an intellectual disposition or a passive mood. It involved the entire person.

Testimony is a verbal, coherent, and rational expression of personal praise. In a typical testimony, praise was given to God for both material and spiritual blessings. As a rule, the material and spiritual were kept in balance and proportion. The testimonies focused on even minute aspects of life and lifted them up as instances of divine intervention and help. The aim of the testimony was to give glory to God for what Jesus had done for the individual. But in addition to that, there was something called a "word of wisdom." A word of wisdom in a testimony could range from exhortation to glorification. If it was exhortation, it was for edification and could be a personal testimony of what God had done for the individual. It was not intended as a short discourse but rather as the telling of what God had done.

---

81   W.E.B.Dubois, *The Souls of Black Folk* (New York: Fawcett, 1961), 10.

"Testifying was considered a great privilege; one could give individual expression like a song of their choice."[82] In testimony, ordinary matters, like waking in the morning, having food to eat, having a right mind, and so on, were lifted beyond the mundane realm. The congregation was reminded that these blessings were not to be taken for granted, for they came directly from God, and at the very moment those at the service were enjoying them. In some instances, the divine intervention to which the testimony bore witness was so pointed and clear that it was placed in the category of "miracle."

Dancing or shouting would sometimes bleed from the praise and testimony service. While singing and hand clapping were permitted to all, dancing and other forms of ecstasy were reserved for those with a certain degree of spiritual attainment. These were signs of fullness of the Spirit, or Spirit possession.

The highest point in praise was ecstasy. This was the point at which all acts of praise found their fulfillment, for at this point worshipers are no longer themselves. Where spiritual ecstasy overflows, we find ourselves so overjoyed that our feet are employed and we call it dance—without a partner of course. This is widely practiced among Pentecostals, and believers are the richer for doing so. Pentecostals understand their dancing as giving glory to God. Also this sometimes was called spontaneous interruption. The act of worship and praise was no longer to be attributed to the individual: through the Spirit, God had made a visitation and was present for the bestowal of blessings.

The devotional service previously described is a part of what is known as "old-time religion."[83] William Harrison Pipes stated in Harriette Pipes McAdoo's book *Black Families,*

---

82   C. Eric Lincoln and Lawrence H. Mamiya, *The Black Church in the African American Experience* (Durham, NC: Duke University Press, 2001), 45

83   Harriette Pipes McAdoo., ed., *Black Families* (Thousand Oaks: Sage, 1997), 41.

The fundamental reason why the Black man clings to the old-time religion is that he has been without a means of normal outward expression, due to his domination by powers beyond his control—in Africa, under colonial control; in America before the Civil war, the institution of slavery; in America today (especially in the "Black Belt" and to a lesser degree in other parts of the United States), the plantation system and/or "divine white right." In Africa and in America many Blacks have made their adjustment to an "impossible world" by means of an emotional escape—the frenzy and shouting of old-time religion. . . . Besides the religious motive, the chief purpose of "old-time black devotional setting" appears to be to "stir up," to excite from an "impossible world." The old-time purpose of persuading people to come to Jesus is still present in varying degrees, but the emphasis here seems to be a secondary one.[84]

It is from this type of old-time religion that the earliest black Methodist Church grew. "Richard Allen and Absalom Jones saw the creeds and ordinances of an ecclesiastical establishment as irrelevant to the spiritual, moral, and material needs of the community. Allen's vision was of a well ordered, but flexible, spirit-filled, community-oriented church that could move immediately into the arena of the movement for freedom and equality. Allen stated that more than anything else he wanted spirited preaching and singing, with congregational participation and the freedom of black worship evolving out of its African background."[85] Throughout his life he was convinced that Methodism came closest to the form of worship desired by blacks, and it was obvious to him that he could not worship as he pleased at St. George's.

84   McAdoo, ed., *Black Families,* 42-43.
85   Wilmore, *Black Religion and Black Radicalism,* 105.

"Therefore, when Allen saw 'a large field open in seeking and instructing my African brethren,'"[86] only a few of whom were attending public worship anywhere, he brought them together in prayer meetings in his own house. When he and Absalom Jones were finally forced from St. George's as they knelt in prayer, they did not immediately establish a competing congregation but what amounted to a Christian association, which they called the Free African Society. Included in it were people of all sorts and conditions, regardless of their religious preferences. Jones stated in his autobiography, "I established prayer meetings; I raised a society in 1786 of forty-two members. I saw the necessity of erecting a place of worship for the colored people. A pattern of religious commitment that has a double focus: free and autonomous worship in the African American tradition, and the solidarity and social welfare of the black community."[87] Several new groups grew from this, and a strong organization, the first national institution organized and controlled by blacks in the United States, evolved out of the spontaneous proliferation in several communities of the Free African Society concept.

Another spontaneous group was "'The Brethren Church.' The River Brethren originated near the Susquehanna River in Lancaster County, Pennsylvania. In about 1780, a small group of Christians led by Jacob Engle met there to form a new fellowship."[88] Most were of Mennonite background but were strongly influenced by the Brethren (Dunker) movement and the Pennsylvania German revivalists that later became the United Brethren Church. The River Brethren developed a unique blending of Christian practices from these three sources. In the 1850s the River Brethren divided into three groups: the Brethren in Christ, the United Zion Church (sounds like A.M. Zion in the black church) and the Old Order River Brethren. There are currently Old Order River Brethren congregations

---

86   Wilmore, *Black Religion and Black Radicalism*, 105-6.
87   Wilmore, *Black Religion and Black Radicalism*, 107.
88   "Church of the Brethren," http://www.brethren.org/

(often called simply River Brethren) in Lancaster and Franklin Counties, Pennsylvania, and in Dallas County, Iowa. York County, Pennsylvania, played an important part in the early history of the group, which is why the River Brethren are sometimes referred to as the "Yorker" Brethren Church.

The life and practices of the Brethren Church center on living as a brotherhood and practicing biblical principles in their everyday lives. The teachings of Jesus in His Sermon on the Mount, including the call for nonresistance to enemies, are emphasized. These beliefs call for honest relationships with neighbors and fellow workers, daily family worship, careful nurture of children, respect for the elderly, helping, visiting, and counseling each other, and volunteering to help the poor or victims of natural disasters. Worship services are central to brotherhood life. Three-hour Sunday morning services include testimonies (as in UHC devotional style of worship) from members and preaching from the plural ministry. Special meetings include love feasts (Communion), councils, harvest meetings, prayer meetings, Bible studies, singings, and youth meetings. Meetings usually are held at members' homes or in rented community buildings. The singing is a cappella and is characterized by a slow, regular cadence.

It is truly amazing to remember that the services in some of the United Holy Churches were, like those of the Brethren Church, three hours long and with slow-cadence songs similar to those of call-and-response type devotional-style songs. The Brethren churches, like the black church, including the UHC, were regulated in their place of worship because of the their style of worship. Often the lack of musicians caused a cappella means to be employed, but it would sound like heaven because of the unity within the worship service. The revivals, which were another name for harvest meetings, would sometimes last to twelve and one in the morning. Prayer meetings and Bible studies would take place the same night, with prayer being the first hour and then Bible study for the next two hours. One thing was common and took place in every setting, and that was singing and dancing before the Lord. This type of worshiping could go on for hours at a time. One can see that the Brethren Church understood the suffering and pain of being confined to a lower or outer limit of social standing to which the UHC and the broader black church were accustomed.

The early a cappella singing of the Brethren Church mirrored a great part of early black church history and slave singing. Wilmore, in *Black Religion and Black Radicalism,* says that it was in the south under the auspices of the "invisible Institution" that the enthusiastic, exciting traits of black religion were most pronounced.[89] In their secret meetings, the slaves worshiped with heartfelt singing, and within the black church rhythm was a must. In *Black Skin White Masks,* Fanon states, "In the face of this affective ankylosis of the white man, it is understandable that I could have made up my mind to utter my Negro cry. Little by little, putting out pseudopodia here and there, I secreted a race. And that race staggered under the burden of a basic element. What was it? Rhythm!"[90] Wilmore helps us to see that a profound example of spontaneous worship developed with the slave community that truly released the consciousness of man.

Sally K. Gallagher, from Oregon State University, presented the results of her research in an article titled, "Building Traditions: Comparing Space, Ritual, and Community in Three congregations."[91] She addressed "the question of how local congregations embody and reflect particular sets of religious goods—both a distinctive sense of community and services, as well as a theologically-based vision of the good through the articulation of particular sets of ideals and practices." She stated,

---

89 Wilmore, *Black Religion and Black Radicalism,* 36.
90 Frantz Fanon, *Black Skin, White Masks* (New York: Grove Press, 1967), 122.
91 Sally K. Gallagher, "Building Traditions: Comparing Space, Ritual, and Community in Three Congregations," *Review of Religious Research* 47:1 (2005): 70-85.

My central concern is to explore how the buildings in which people worship, the ritual movements of the congregation, and the pastor's vision of what it means for the church to be "a body" communicate distinctive and coherent sets of theological propositions about what is "good." In doing so, I seek to put theological tradition at the center of the analysis—highlighting the salience of diverse beliefs and styles of worship that give meaning to membership and character to congregational life. My primary thesis is that, although denominations may be declining as a marker of religious identity, churches continue to be places in which individuals are offered opportunity to locate and experience a sense of identity and community framed by distinctive streams of theological tradition.[92]

Gallagher touches on a Presbyterian church that embraced a diversity of worship similar to that of the United Holy Church. She shows in her research that at one time there was a separation in First Prebyterian's worship service because of age difference, but the church showed that a balanced style of worship or a revitalization of worship can take place in a congregation. Until recently, this church worshiped as a single group, with older members seated in the center, surrounded by couples with children. Today,

Worship services ... are a rich array of diverse elements—complex programs that begin with a pastor's greeting and move through nineteen different segments (reading, prayers, announcements, sermon, etc.) before concluding an hour and fifteen minutes later. Music in a diversity of styles is an important part of this congregation's identity. Services typically include an instrumental prelude (on the organ or grand piano, with an occasional instrumental quartet), an informal "gathering song,"

---

92   Gallagher, "Building Traditions," 70.

two hymns, a praise chorus and a choral anthem. Lay readers lead the congregation from a central lectern, reading from the psalms a call to worship, selections from the old and new testaments, leading a corporate prayer of confession, announcing forgiveness, and directing the congregation to greet those seated around them (a "passing of the peace" in which either "peace of the Lord" or "good morning" suffice as a way to connect with other people). ... Much of the informal work of the church takes place during the half hour before and after the service as people exchange news, update health reports, and organize volunteers, materials and schedules for later in the week.[93]

Gallagher made a comparison between First Presbyterian and Valley Baptist Church, which reflects several aspects of the United Holy Church forms of worship. "Valley Baptist is in many ways the mirror image of First Presbyterian," and it also shows the need of revitalizing worship in order to be inclusive. Gallagher states,

> This conservative Baptist congregation is located literally and figuratively on the wrong side of the tracks. It is largely working class—reflective of the town's economic base—and includes a small but growing number of the recently homeless, recovering substance abusers, single mothers and marginally employed. Like First Presbyterian, it was a graying congregation until the arrival of a new, younger and energetic pastor three years ago. His arrival brought numerous changes to the church's organization and culture. As Pastor Mark explains, "This is a very old church that had experienced significant decline and a lot of liabilities; old constituency, old neighborhood, old facility, bad reputation, significant flight out of the church in terms of young people. I knew that it was a tough situation that would require drastic

---

93   Gallagher, "Building Traditions," 81.

turnaround and that brings with it a certain level of organizational trauma. So before we accepted the call, I told them we'd be making a lot of changes to the way they'd been doing things—the music would be totally changed, the service would be simplified, and ministries to unchurched people made high priority."[94]

The changes have indeed been many. Central to the worship service are music and preaching, and the organ has been replaced by electric guitars, keyboards, and drums, a change some older members were not happy with. However, the transition has been relatively smooth, due in large part to the congregation's desire to incorporate younger people and their prior agreement to significant changes. Pastor Mark's wife, Sara, has given leadership to women's small groups and the children's ministry, adding "to a sense of revitalized and relevant activities at the church. VBC is thoroughly evangelical, with its Bible-centered, entertaining, pragmatic and personal approach to what it means to be a Christian and a part of the church."[95]

Gallagher notes that many of the elements of the worship service at Valley Baptist are similar to those at First Presbyterian, including a brief welcome, an offering (though visitors are discouraged from giving!), and testimonies on occasion. At Valley Baptist, however, the worship is much less formal.

> For nearly half an hour, the congregation stands and sings contemporary worship music, the lyrics of which are projected on the big screen at the front of the sanctuary. Some periodically raise their hands, most clap or tap their feet to the upbeat rhythms of the music. Songs are simple and encouraging; addressing God directly ... and emphasizing the hope, peace

---

94   Gallagher, "Building Traditions," 81.
95   Gallagher, "Building Traditions," 82.

and strength that are available through a personal relationship with Jesus Christ.[96]

Fervent spirit, manifestation of Holy Spirit charismata, spontaneity, enthusiasm, Bible-centeredness, and emphasis on the immanence, or closeness, of God— "these are the prominent features of the ecstatic worship to be experienced at the black Assemblies of God (AOG) church. The AOG was later referred to as 'Fire Baptized' Assembly of God Church, a fitting appellation, given the fiery, almost frenzied nature of services there."[97]

The order of their service is similar to that of the United Holy Church, and they constantly heard some of the same remarks, such as, "I couldn't worship at a Pentecostal church because I need something with structure."[98] It is a common misconception that there is no order or orderliness in a Pentecostal worship service. Their services start with a choir marching in, sometimes robed, and at other times dressed color coordinated. After the choir reaches the choir loft and concludes the processional song, spontaneous praise breaks out; and the devotional leader leads the church in a time of devotion, praise, and singing, which is the first segment of worship. Congregants clap, cheer, and lift their hands in adoration and surrender to Christ, whom they consider the honored guest at worship, present by way of the Holy Spirit. The devotional leader will give what might be considered a "spiritual pep talk,"[99] and worshipers can be heard speaking in tongues, with others praising God in English. Some worshipers dance in the Spirit. This time of devotion may last for a period of thirty

---

96 Gallagher, "Building Traditions," 101.

97 L. Grant McClung, Jr., ed., *Azusa Street and Beyond: Pentecostal Missions and Church Growth in the Twentieth Century* (South Plainfield, NJ: Bridge, 1986), 71-73.

98 McClung, Jr., ed., *Azusa Street and Beyond*, 75.

99 Brenda Eatman Aghahowa, *Praising in Black and White: Unity and Diversity in Christian Worship* (Cleveland: United Church Press, 1996), 87-89.

minutes, and it is followed by a prayer and Scripture reading, while congregants are still standing.

The following is an order of worship service for both the UHC and the Fire Baptized.

Morning Worship of Fire Baptized	**Morning Worship of UHC**
Choir Processional	Devotion
Period of Devotion/Praise	Call to Worship
Responsive Scripture Reading	Processional
Time of Holy Hugs/Love Fest (Not in UHC Program)	Hymn
Announcements	Reading of Holy Scripture
Offering	Request for Prayer
Choral Selections (A&B)	Pastoral Prayer
Sermon	Hymn
Altar Call	Offering
Benediction	Announcements
	Anthem, Spiritual, or Hymn
	Sermon
	Invitational
	Doxology
	Benediction

As I think about the United Holy Church "Devotional Service," I am struck by the fact that it reflects a personal relationship to Christ. There is a collective catharsis that meets the needs of individuals to release tension or distressful emotion, thereby delivering a sense of motivation to recapture one's identity and to express oneself freely. The churches mentioned above have captured the spirit of the Holiness-Pentecostal Movement of the late nineteenth century, emerging out of Methodism and John

Wesley's search for spiritual perfection, which was carried one step further by the Pentecostalists with their stress on another blessing of the Spirit (with its evidence of glossolalia, interpretation, and prophesying, or other "gifts of the Spirit").

As is the case in this day, it was not uncommon in the past for one parent in a family to be Methodist and the other to be Holiness, with the children going to both churches. Or, as was the case in rural areas, each denominational church would have preaching on one Sunday out of the month, but everyone in the community frequented all the churches and participated in all as members. Even more, they joined in and produced common strands of worship, and they all became familiar at the popular level with one another's doctrines. In some cases there developed a "blend" that was shared by all.

For all practical purposes, what one had in those open communities was the precursor to the "blended worship" that is so characteristic of contemporary patterns. This can be seen in churches that have adopted an "upbeat" tone to their worship and in others that have rejected the traditional denominational labels altogether. This train of thought brings to mind the view of "twoness" by DuBois. Dubois wrote, "One ever feels his twoness—an American, a Negro; two souls, two thoughts; two unreconciled strivings; two warring ideals in one dark body."[100] One had to exist in two distinct worlds: one black because of race and identity and one white because of the wider culture, and the economic, political, educational, and social systems in America.

This view also brings to mind DuBois' words on the search for identity, which essentially was a personal, intellectual enterprise in self-clarification: "The struggle of the black masses to achieve identity has been a gut struggle in the pursuit of group recognition and dignification."[101] When the black church became clear that the white man's Christianity could not or would not afford the inclusive cover of human dignity required, it was obvious that

---

100 Dubois, *The Souls of Black Folk*, xxii.
101 Dubois, *The Souls of Black Folk*, 5.

some other means would have to be discovered or invented. Slavery provided no institutional opportunities even remotely available to black dignification, and the prevailing image of the church was of a white institution substantially accommodated to black debasement.

Because of the debasement and lack of opportunities of free expression, an alternative church was born, an "underground church" dubbed by history "the invisible institution."[102] This was a black church that developed outside and independently of the white man's church. Ultimately it would give definition to the individual black person and would become a powerful force in the reclamation of personal identity. This invisible institution was the church of the field hands. But in the outdoor tabernacle of the swamps, the sand hills, and the backwoods, the ambience was different. The music, the prayers, and the testimonials were rooted in the day-to-day experiences of plantation life, and the prevailing message was not "obey your masters," but "God wants you . . . free!"[103] To be wanted was a powerful, unaccustomed affirmation of self-estimate. To be free, like other people, could only mean that God wanted them to be responsible—to Him, for where there is no freedom the notion of responsibility is mockery. Through the eyes of one desiring freedom, this devotional style allows a glance through the window panes of being wanted and can birth true identity, the unfettered projection of the self, which is the inalienable corollary of freedom, if not indeed its first function. Identity is the projection of somebodyness, the sum of a differentiated, individuated human being, a person with inalienable rights to testify, sing, pray, clap, and shout on a spontaneous basis through a song, then and now, during devotional services.

---

102 Lincoln and Mamiya, *The Black Church in the African American Experience*, 5.
103 Lincoln and Mamiya, *The Black Church in the African American Experience*, 4.

If anybody asks you
Who I am
Who I am
Who I am
If anybody asks you
Who I am
You can tell'em
I'm a child of God![104]

The history of the American Negro is a history of strife. The black church helped by rendering a stage to produce freedom and identity. Freedom has always been an intimate concern of the black church; and in its pilgrimage toward that goal, the much-used songs of Charles Wesley seemed increasingly inexpressive of the urgencies felt by black people. The UHC helped to deliver a sense of identity captured through the means of spontaneous devotional worship, singing those songs like "If anybody ask you who I am just tell them I'm a child of God." There is identity through spontaneous worship.

---

104 Nix, *Songs of Zion*, 74.

Chapter 4

METHODOLOGY OF RESEARCH

"God's gift to his sorrowing creatures is to give
the joy worthy of their destiny."
Johann Sebastian Bach, 1685-1750

The faith movements described in chapter 3 reflect shared priorities
with the United Holy Church "devotional services." Despite the
diversity of ways Christians flesh out worship in actual ritual
performance from denomination to denomination, from church
to church, and from culture to culture, there is some unity in the
form and common purposes, and it is seen as useful and needful to
those particular organizations. This chapter will describe a survey
of bishops, preachers/pastors, and lay members in the UHC that
was taken to determine their views of the value of devotional
services within their congregations and to see if contemporary
praise and worship is the choice of twenty-first-century United
Holy Church parishioners.

The study describes the motivating factors behind the choice
of either the traditional style worship or the contemporary style
of praise and worship. This chapter will deal with the site of
the survey, the nature of the study, a description of the study, a
sample population for the study, data collection procedure, and
the analysis of the survey.

Site of the Survey

The Southern District Convocation is a part of the United Holy Church of America, Inc., an African American denomination founded in 1886. This organization was selected because of its many years of existence and because of its ability to recover and spring back after a very traumatic split.[105] The headquarters for the Southern District Convocation (SDC) of the United Holy Church is located in Goldsboro, North Carolina, which was this study's focal point. The majority of the surveys were taken from leaders within the SDC. Reconciliation with regard to the worship style is needed because the reunification of the church brought contemporary-style praise and worship into several of the UHC churches. This caused some conflict within the body.

It is important to note that for fifty years I have been affiliated with the UHC—in childhood and some of my young adult life and now my adult life—and devotional-style worship has lived throughout my entire life. Now I serve as a pastor, a district elder, and a member of the board of presbytery within the SDC, and it is my observation that there is a great need for a coming together of worship styles in the church.

The surveys were taken September 23, 2009 during our annual convocation of the Southern District. The convocation is an eight-day time of elegant, formal, majestic worship. During this time of worship, the 180 churches that make up the Southern District Convocation are presented and report to the leadership. From the opening Sunday, we are able to see the prescribed denominational liturgy; what is communicated in worship by architecture, vestments, ministerial style, and the like; the resulting tone of worship; and strengths and limitations of worship and related issues.

---

105 The United Holy Church split in 1977 because of differences among leadership. The UHC remained separated until May 2000, when a reunification took place.

The opening Sunday the gathering totals around two thousand participants. Members are largely black decision makers, including elected officials, lawyers, educators, financiers, entrepreneurs, farmers, and other professionals.[106] The congregation is aging, with two-thirds of the members being sixty years of age or older. The church struggles to attract and keep younger members. (I often wonder if it's the traditional worship style that hinders those efforts.) The exact ratio of women to men is not known, but—as is the case in most black churches—there seem to be more women than men. The Southern District and the United Holy Church as a whole are gender inclusive. Throughout the worship practices, the UHC continually affirms women worshipers (by allowing them opportunities to hold leadership positions, to minister during major conferences, to lead worship, and to pastor), both explicitly and implicitly, as first-class citizens in God's family and in God's ministry. They are affirmed explicitly by the bishop's consistent use of inclusive language.

The testing site location for the survey was United Christian College (UCC), which is the UHC's Bible training school for preachers and Christian workers. The survey was tested at this location August 24, 2009 to insure this format would work. UCC was organized in 1926, and it still provides training for all the ministers in the Southern District Convocation. United Christian College also holds a major place in black history. William Turner, a son of the United Holy Church, an instructor at Duke University, and a notable Christian writer, observes,

> During the height of the civil rights movement of the 1960's, members of the United Holy Church were significant participants in the historic events that took place in Greensboro, North Carolina. In Goldsboro, North Carolina, students of the United Holy Church's school initiated attempts to

---

106 Holiness Union-Statistical Data of United Holy Church-Volume MMIX: No. II, April 2008

eat at the counter of the Woolworth store, and the United Christian College became the center from which action emanated in that eastern North Carolina city.[107]

Nature of the Survey

This study includes surveys and interviews with bishops, pastors, and lay members of the Southern District Convocation of the United Holy Church of America and a few interviews with individuals from other parts of the United Holy Church. What do they feel worship should be and do? Do members of the two contrasting views reveal any unity or consensus of opinion, or only diversity and division concerning their worship needs and preferences?

Information was collected on their choice of the traditional-style devotional worship or the contemporary style of worship. The survey served for the development of an understanding of each individual's experience with worship within the denomination. Each participant's responses and descriptions of the worship style of choice were compared with other interviews taken. This comparison allowed the researcher to isolate facts pertaining to the organization's preference of worship style.

Description of the Survey

The survey took the form of a questionnaire that examines how pastors and lay members feel the traditional format of devotional service works in their services. Each survey also asked how each individual felt about the modern-day contemporary praise and

---

107 William C. Turner Jr., *The United Holy Church of America* (Piscataway, NJ: Gorgias Press, 2006), 56.

worship in their worship services and whether they felt this or the traditional devotional service most met their spiritual needs.[108]

I distributed a three-part survey instrument to all participating members to supplement my own observation and scores of informal conversations with worshipers.[109] Respondents were informed that the survey responses would be treated confidentially, and signing their names to the survey was optional.

The initial section asks respondents to provide demographic information in order to enhance understanding of how socioeconomic factors affect worship. Worshipers are asked their age, gender, race, marital status, family size, years at their local UHC church, occupation, and whether they tithe consistently (optional).

In the second section, worshipers are asked to share their theological understandings of the following basic Christian concepts: God, Christ, the Holy Spirit, sin, salvation, the body of Christ, and the Bible. Next, respondents are asked to identify the sources of their religious training, such as Bible study, sermons, books, etc. Worshipers also are asked to describe briefly their spiritual pilgrimage.

In the final section of the survey, participants are asked to evaluate and describe the strengths and weaknesses of their worship services, to compare devotional-style worship to contemporary praise and worship formats, to compare their church to other churches they have visited, and to make any comments they would like regarding their worship.

Analyzing these survey responses will help to address with understanding what makes for a fulfilling worship experience from the perspectives of the laypersons (non-leaders in the church) and how their expectations jibe with leadership. I am not a trained statistician, so my data analysis is more qualitative than quantitative. Still, the survey results are both revealing and

---

108 See the appendix, which reproduces the survey.
109 September 21, 2009 at Love Temple Goldsboro, NC administered by Charles E. Lewis.

instructive. Proverbs tells us, "And with all you have gotten, get understanding (discernment, comprehension, and interpretation)" (4:7 AMP).

Description of Site Selection of the Study

The Southern District Convocation of the United Holy Church of America, Inc. is a part of the UHC, a diverse African American group founded in 1886 with churches in eight different countries. This organization was selected for this survey and study for the following reasons.

> SDC is a non-secular African American organization that is the mother district of the UHC, which was divided and experienced significant conflict.

> SDC is a non-secular African American organization that overcame problems and reunified with the UHC.

> SDC was in the midst of reunification at the time, and the leaders of the organization welcomed the historical process of reunification.

> SDC has reunified on paper with the UHC, but worship is still divided. Worship within SDC congregations is the area this survey will focus on.

A Sample Population for the Survey

An interview and survey were given to the general president of the United Holy Church of America, who stated that he feels that the traditional devotional service needs to be monitored closely because it has the tendency to take up a lot of time and causes people to be turned off somewhat with the service. He felt that both styles encompass a deep theological grounding and can make a dramatic impact on any worship setting.[110] A written survey was given to the district minister of music, and his response was that it takes both the traditional devotion and contemporary praise and worship to make the service go well.[111] He feels that a proper blending will allow all saints to feel as if they are a part of the worship service.

Surveys were given to pastors on the board of presbytery. This board consists of twelve pastors taken from different subdistricts throughout the Southern District Convocation. Their responsibility is to license the pastors of the district. The survey showed that half of the board members were for contemporary-style praise and worship and half were for the traditional style. Those who preferred the traditional style did so mainly because they felt it represents who the UHC is as a church and because the contemporary style encourages entertainment in the worship service, and the people need to be a part of the worship experience rather than entertained.[112]

During the annual convocation, thirty-eight lay members were selected at random to complete the survey. This represented about 10 percent of the 350 delegates who might attend morning worship during convocation. They felt that contemporary praise and worship created the appropriate atmosphere for worship and allowed everyone the opportunity to sing together and not alone, therefore promoting a more community atmosphere of worship. The lay members felt that traditional-style worship allowed individuals to put on a show of their own by over singing and

---

110 Bishop Elijah Williams, interview by Charles Lewis, September 23, 2009, Love Temple, Goldsboro, NC.

111 James Bigalow, September 21, 2009, Love Temple Goldsboro, NC

112 All the results mentioned here and hereafter come from the "Biblical Worship Survey" conducted September 21-25, 2009, at Love Temple Goldsboro North Carolina.

giving testimonies that glorified themselves rather than giving the glory to God.

There were eighteen pastors selected at random to take the survey, which was 10 percent of the pastors in the Southern District. The churches in the Southern District are labeled as small, medium, and large, and six pastors were selected from each group. The pastors with the smaller congregations generally felt that the traditional-style worship worked well in all their services because it added an element of unity and bonded people together. These pastors felt that it brought the "frenzy" to their worship services and added a deeper spiritual element to their worship experience. Pastors of both the medium and large congregations expressed their appreciation for the freedom of everyone to minister in the devotional service but believed that contemporary praise and worship works better with time. They also felt that contemporary worship sometimes tends to leave out the free moving of the Holy Ghost. They believe in structure but not in putting God in a box—though the structure saves time. This thought pattern is more common in the smaller churches because medium and large churches experience the 11 a.m. – 3 p.m. worship services due to the lengthy devotional service.

Survey Sampling: SDC United Holy Church Worship Style Survey

One of the basic features of church life in the United Holy Church is the proliferation of worship and music. This survey examines the devotional-style worship in the United Holy Church, which is spontaneous, versus the modern-day contemporary praise and worship style, which is a more structured style with less spontaneity.

In the twenty-first century, the church needs an extra edge, and many have found that high-quality worship can make the difference between winning and retaining members or losing them. Research has shown that churches that employ a more biblically based worship gain member satisfaction, loyalty, and retention. Cornelius Plantinga Jr. and Sue A. Rozeboom, in their book entitled *Discerning the Spirits--A Guide to Thinking About Christian Worship Today,* share insight into this concept.

> Worship planners specifically target three or four identity groupings in their own church, and worship planning resources come with predefined audiences in mind. Church officers sometimes try to prevent the quarrels with a roundtable strategy of equal recognition of all. We're keeping everybody happy they say. Different strokes for different folks, they say, so let's try to blend those strokes and keep our folks.[113]

Therefore, by determining which style produces the highest perceived value, we can provide the knowledge to both correct deficiencies in today's ministries and assist in building in the weaving and wonder of biblical worship.

Data Collection Procedure

The worship surveys were passed out during our annual convocation of the Southern District Convocation of the United Holy Church of America, where all the pastors and lay members gather for a weeklong service and where each style of worship could be evaluated. These services take place in September of each year. On September 21, 2009, during the first morning services of the convocation, approximately one hundred surveys were distributed, with the General Bishop of the Convocation receiving the first copy of the survey and the bishops and pastors, including the minister of music of the Southern District, receiving

113 Cornelius Plantinga Jr. and Sue A. Rozeboom, *Discerning the Spirits* (Grand Rapids: Eerdmans, 2003), 99.

the next forty-nine copies of the survey. Thirty-eight surveys were given to lay members and twelve to the board of presbytery. The first day of the convocation is always on a Monday. The morning services throughout the week feature the traditional-style devotional worship beginning with prayer, Scripture, spontaneous singing, and spontaneous testimonies. At the afternoon services, contemporary praise and worship is combined with the opportunity for worshipers to testify. The evening services feature praise and worship only.

Instructions were given to all participants. Some of the people hesitated and wondered if trouble would follow, while others received the survey without any hesitation. All participants were given the surveys and instructed to return all surveys, completed or not, to the one who administered the survey on that Friday of the Convocation, September 25, 2009, following the morning worship service. A total of 95 percent of the surveys were returned.

Analysis of Survey

While relatively small, the sampling of the general bishop and bishops and leaders of the Southern District Convocation of the United Holy Church is rich and meaningful. All respondents were male and senior citizens by society's definition of a senior citizen, which starts at the age of sixty-two. Five of the seven respondents in this group who completed the survey felt that traditional-style worship fits their spiritual appetite best. The others simply described themselves as favoring a blended worship, stating that they could live with both and do not have a preference.

Students from a Christian Worship class at United Christian College were given the task of determining the best style of worship for the survey participants, starting with the surveys of pastors and ministers of music. This was to be completed after the students read Robert Webber's *Worship Old & New*. The students' analysis concluded that it would be best if a blended style of worship were utilized for the services because the surveys showed that everyone favored combination-style worship. All students agreed it would be the best course of action, because utilizing the old traditional style along with the new contemporary would allow the community of worshipers to experience a more diverse format of worship.

The students also completed an analysis of the board of presbytery's surveys. In response to the questions about worship choices, members of the board for fifteen years said, "Strength of devotional service is that there still remains the individual testimony in the UHC. The weakness for the contemporary praise and worship is that everybody doesn't know those songs."[114]

A much newer and younger member of the board said, "The strength of the services today is the contemporary music for worship. Often at the end of the worship service it's very easy to find contemporary praise and worship songs to fit for altar calls."[115]

The crucial issue for many seems to be expressed best by two other members, one female and one male pastor, who felt that services utilizing devotional style and contemporary are often spiritually uplifting enough; however, devotional has the tendency to be too long, which can have a negative impact on the entire worship service if there are new worshipers, because of the time it requires. Contemporary praise and worship allows for, and requires, greater time management.

The students' analysis of the surveys showed that though the board was split down the middle, most of the board members leaned to the traditional style of worship. The students stated that they would utilize the devotional, traditional-style worship during their prayer and Bible study service and inform the congregation that during the prayer and Bible study, testimony service would be allowed so that those who felt the need to give their testimonies

---

114 Interview taken by Charles Lewis on September 26, 2009 of the Board of Presbytery of the Southern District Convocation of the United Holy Church.

115 Interview taken by Charles Lewis on September 26, 2009.

could do so during that time. However, during their Sunday morning services, there would be no testimony or devotional-style singing done; rather it would be a structured order of praise and worship with a team that had practiced during the week to lead the congregation into worship. By conducting their services with this format, all members would have a chance to experience their preferred style of worship. In addition, the attendance at Bible study possibly would increase, and those who are mainly for contemporary worship would be able to see if the testimony time is something they would like to share in.

The surveys of the lay members of the United Holy Church Southern District were the next to be analyzed. The lay members included people who had been a part of UHC all of their lives and some who has just arrived in the UHC, yet it was interesting that all the lay members felt the same about the worship style.

Twenty-four of the thirty-eight respondents rated the contemporary praise and worship model services as good to excellent, while the remaining fourteen rated the contemporary fair or gave no rating. Regardless of the rating given, at least three points were hammered home as worshiper responses were considered as a group.

First, members said that more attention is paid to personal spirituality in devotional worship settings and less to corporate worship, when fellowship and relationship are central concepts in Sunday gatherings. Contemporary-style worship embraces corporate unity, which should be the heartbeat of the church.

Second, with respect to music, while contemporary praise and worship is superior in its performance, the fourteen who preferred the devotional service, as well as some of the twenty-four who preferred the contemporary service, stated that they wished to sing familiar songs from the black religious experience and not the "strange" songs mostly heard in the contemporary praise and worship.

Finally, the lay members' surveys stated that devotional-style worship prolonged the service, often being justified under the banner of the Holy Spirit. It causes the entire body and worship service to appear ill equipped for Christian service.

The consensus of the lay members was that praise and worship is best for corporate worship and in turn enhances their own personal spiritual growth and worship experience. It was interesting to see that while the majority embraced praise and worship, most members felt they should not change the style of worship for their church to be entirely praise and worship because the majority of the members of the church are seniors, who were raised on devotional services. Therefore, they agreed that the contemporary praise and worship should be carried out on youth Sunday and traditional praise and worship utilized in their regular worship services.

My Conclusion

Let us now consider what the survey results suggest in more detail. The surveys reveal overwhelming satisfaction with the worship as currently shaped and with the overall quality of communal feeling at the church. In all, 94 percent of respondents rated the devotional-style worship service good, close to excellent, or excellent.

While survey participants were extremely satisfied with the worship as currently shaped and none of their spiritual needs were unmet, several embraced the praise and worship offered in some churches. These and other voices plead for more attention to practical issues of worship (such as time restraints) in the traditional devotional worship service, which includes a unit of testimony services in which individual worshipers can stand and give personal testimonies about how God has intervened in their lives. Some worshipers felt that this is a valuable part of their worship service and cannot be left out; but others stated that it took up too much time, causing the service to drag on, with people at times testifying about things that did not bring any glory to God. Members said they wanted and needed encouragement from that type of service, but it should be done in a smaller setting such as midweek services, where time is not such a factor. There were also those who felt that testimonies and the devotional style should be expelled altogether (this was only 5 percent of the participants). The survey also revealed that there are some who feel that contemporary praise and worship should be used in all services and others who consider contemporary praise and worship a form of entertainment.

As I looked at all those surveyed, it was very surprising to see that a lot of the members of the SDC of the United Holy Church desire to maintain the traditional-style worship, even when a part of them like the contemporary praise and worship. There is loyalty to the traditional-style worship because some people fear the departure from tradition would do more harm than good.

Also, the surveys show that a balance is needed within our worship services. All survey participants were willing to use all methods of worship, even if they were not in total agreement with one particular style. Survey participants made mention of the need for spontaneity within the worship service, and the only place that most feel spontaneity can be utilized is in the traditional devotional style. Based on the opinions gained from the survey, reconciliation and revitalization has taken place in some congregations, but it is not seen throughout the entire United Holy Church.

I close this section with a statement from a survey participant. She said, "Sometimes I feel the services might be a little lengthy, but when I look back, I can never see anything that wasn't necessary or that didn't minister."[116] It appears that without knowing it, she was wrestling here, at least in part, with the issue of balancing devotional and contemporary worship. I hope that many of the insights here have served as spiritual dynamite for many—possibly exploding certain myths and misconceptions in

---

116 Survey from Geneva Coley a mother in a local United Holy Church Goldsboro, North Carolina. The survey was taken September 2009, during the annual SDC Convocation.

Charles E. Lewis Sr.

a variety of areas. So let us for the moment, set aside controversies related to devotional-style worship and contemporary worship and return our focus to the major aim of this work: to enhance unity by promoting an appreciation of the strengths of both styles of worship.

Chapter 5

OUTCOMES

"God of grace and God of Glory, on your people pour your power; crown your ancient church's story; Bring its bud to glorious flow'r. Grant us wisdom; grant us courage For the facing of this hour, For the facing of this hour."
Harry Emerson Fosdick, 1878-1969

Today, churches across the country and within the United Holy Church are torn between the tug of tradition and the pull of style. Seniors want harmony; boomers and X'ers want beat. Each has difficulty accepting the other with enthusiasm. Believers must understand that worship often is formed as much by culture as it is by theological considerations. In seeking to improve the worship of the SDC of the UHC, participants must make sure that the Bible is directing their desire for change and that people are conscious and aware of how their interpretations and evaluations are being culturally conditioned. I hope that the outcome of this work will be revitalization and restoration so that the "devotional-style worship" with its dependence upon spontaneous worship will aid the younger generation and cause them to understand their heritage. I also hope that this revitalization concept will bring some stability to the general body of the United Holy Church by bringing back into focus how so many of the past saints within the United Holy Church endured painful suffering through this therapeutic process of spontaneous worship. This project will give hope for revitalizing devotional-style worship so that worshipers will not simply communicate the gospel to people but also celebrate the gospel before the people. Revitalization and reconciliation is needed, with the understanding that worship that is strictly contemporary will become dated very quickly. Therefore, we must move toward total reconciliation and revitalization of spontaneous-style, devotional worship within the United Holy Church, because "worship that is not rooted in any particular historic tradition will often lack the critical distance to critique and avoid the excesses and distorted sinful elements of the particular surrounding present culture."[117]

The Wesleyan tradition, which spawned the Holiness Movement, holds to a fourfold evaluation process for worship. Any particular style or format is evaluated by using four basic sources: "scripture, reason, tradition, and experience."[118] The UHC too must utilize some means of gauging the elements of worship and not assume that one form of worship, whether traditional or contemporary, is more pure than the other. Just as it is a lack of humility to disdain tradition, it is also a lack of humility to elevate any particular tradition or culture's way of doing worship above all others.

In Mark 7:8-9 Jesus spoke about the traditions of the Pharisees and scribes, who were "'ditching God's command and taking up the latest fads.' He went on, 'Well, good for you. You get rid of God's command so you won't be inconvenienced in following the religious fashions!'"[119] A refusal to adapt a tradition to new realities

---

117 Pedrito U. Maynard-Reid. *Diverse Worship: African-American, Caribbean & Hispanic Perspectives* (Downers Grove, IL: InterVarsity, 2000), 56.

118 John N. Oswalt. *Called to Be Holy: A Biblical Perspective* (Nappanee, IN: Evangel, 1999), 35.

119 Eugene H. Peterson, *The Message: The Bible in Contemporary Language* (Colorado Springs: NavPress, 2002).

may fall under Jesus' words of condemnation, thus making our favorite human culture into an idol.

I also hope that this project will show the immense need to embrace both styles of worship by revitalizing and reconciling the old so that both believers and seekers will instantly sense a real worship experience. Therefore, we must address the worshipers through revitalization of the spontaneous aspect of devotional service within the United Holy Church.

The subject of worship can and should be addressed from a variety of perspectives, cultural as well as theological. What I present here are the results of others' long experience and reflections on the spontaneous culture and belief systems of worship in the United Holy Church. I will close out this work by looking at items that will allow us to revitalize the worship of the SDC United Holy Church, as well as focus on being culturally conscious, calling this people of God to remembrance, integration, assimilation, denominational loyalty, and acceptance.

Culturally Conscious

One of the last sessions during my doctoral residence stressed the importance of being conscious of one's culture and not throwing away what built the bridge that enabled one to gain what has been accomplished up to the present time. Kathy Black states that culture is "the sum attitudes, customs, and beliefs that distinguishes one group of people from another."[120] I totally agree. The United Holy Church's traditional devotional style distinguishes, not only who we are as a church, but also who we are as a people.

We also understand that culture is transmitted through language, material objects, ritual, institutions, and art from one generation to the next. It is through the devotional-style worship of spontaneous singing, testimonies, prayers from the soul, and dancing in the Spirit that a language for our church is revealed

120 Kathy Black, *Culturally Conscious Worship* (St. Louis: Chalice, 2000), 8.

and a ritual is established that the church can pass on to the next generation. That is why the current leaders must make sure that they are not the generation that buries a heritage.

Being culturally conscious also means taking into account the youth culture, which is very difficult for modern-day worshipers to do, especially when believers are starched into the tradition of old. It is very difficult to understand the language of the youth today and the meanings behind their words. Their music and other things separate them from us, yet the attitudes, customs, and beliefs play a major part in each generation.

A congregation is identified by its behavior patterns. We must be able to move from one group to the other by embracing each view of life and blending the worship styles. One avenue that should allow us to blend together is to remember that afro haircuts, bell-bottom slacks, and platform shoes are no longer in style; but when they were, we blended them into the church and were allowed to worship. Now we are the carriers of the same traditional style of worship that our parents utilized. Therefore, the way to embrace the new is to first remember from where we have come.

Call to Remembrance

"The people of God are to remember God's deeds of salvation and his promise of the land by being grateful and by committing their lives. And they are to come before him with a particular attitude of homage and reverence in the presence of their King."[121] Our first response as a renewed apostolic worshiper is to remember. The Greek word for "remember," or "recalling to mind," is *anamnesis*. Genesis 24:26-27 tells us that when Abraham's servant found a wife for Isaac, he "bowed down and worshiped the Lord, saying, 'Praise be to the Lord.'" His worship was a heartfelt thanksgiving in response to God's provision. This is the attitude God desires in

---

121 Robert E. Webber, *Worship Old & New: A Biblical, Historical, and Practical Introduction* (Grand Rapids: Zondervan, 1994), 27.

response to his acts of salvation. The psalmist declares in Psalm 66:4 that all the earth bows down to God.

Remembering is essential to our sense of identity. Our deepest emotions are intimately linked with how we remember and what we recall. My grandmother is ninety-four years old and has been diagnosed with early stages of dementia and Alzheimer's. She can't seem to remember names or what just happened two seconds ago, but she has no problem remembering songs and testimonies from twenty to thirty years ago. She can sing those devotional songs and still has a desire to give her testimony about the goodness of the Lord. This is why the literal loss of memory by persons in the grip of disease or struck by physical accident has such tragic dimensions. Disoriented stares from loved ones who cannot remember their own names or their relationships to persons, places, and events are profoundly disturbing. People rightly fear the severe loss of personal memory and must be careful not to strip away something that will cause some to become prisoners to their own immediate experience.

When looking at the contemporary movement of praise and worship, worshipers must remember that some years ago Edward Hawkins's "Oh Happy Day" was looked upon as a travesty in the church. The style and the movement by the choir were thought to surely be the downfall of the church, but instead it is a gospel hall-of-fame record now. It delivered a new movement that still has not destroyed the traditional, devotional-style worship but rather has enhanced gospel music. We must open ourselves to all others to be added, for when we do so, we can reconcile with others and revitalize what we have so that all can be a part of the church and find some form of life.

Integration

This is a subject that is very familiar to the black church as a whole and certainly to the United Holy Church. In order for us to be agents of reconciliation and revitalization, the UHC will have to incorporate integration within their churches. Brown v. Board of Education is a very familiar event in the history of America. This Supreme Court decision forced integration in the public school system in 1954. The civil rights movement led by Martin Luther King Jr. was in full swing in the mid 60s, which caused some African Americans to claim their rights to full integration in this society in restaurants, on buses, in schools, and in churches.

The majority of our churches are monoracial (all-black churches/congregants), but within them we do have different beliefs. And as we have focused on throughout this work, those who promote the contemporary worship style can be seen as a different generational group because of a different set of customs and beliefs. The educational differences also bring into place the observance of different customs, beliefs, and language. Therefore, while we may be primarily monoracial, we are different groups and in need of integration.

As a group of monoracial individuals, we must remember what we felt when our beliefs and language were looked down upon; and we must open our hearts and minds to the feelings of others. In the early days of integration, if African Americans were welcomed at all, they had to abide by the rules that were set. If we were allowed in other churches during the flux of integration, we had to abide by the style of worship, music choices, and channels of authority of the dominant culture. We could join as long as we did not make any demands and acted liked the dominant group. And we know that there were African Americans who chose to join all-white churches (for whatever reasons), and other African Americans accused them of "running from their blackness" and betraying their community and called them "oreos" (black on the outside and white on the inside). This caused a migration back to the historical black churches with new ideas and views from other contexts.

African Americans have been the leaders in pioneering the integration of Anglo-European congregations and other groups. Nevertheless, within our church we must engineer integration between contemporary worship and traditional worship because it has caused a great divide within our own walls. It is this division that created an atmosphere of hatred and dissention instead of an atmosphere of worship. What we need within the UHC is a spiritual court decision (a Spirit-led decision made by UHC leadership about worship styles within the body) of the Holy Spirit regarding traditional and contemporary worship that will allow forced integration to happen and will produce love and unity to envelope the body so that revitalization can take place in our worship experience.

Assimilation

"The goal of an assimilation ministry is to help new members move from simply attending to belonging. It is the difference between renting and owning. As leaders, we want our members to accept responsibility and ownership for the church's ministries."[122] If the process of worship style is explained and blended worship demonstrated from the beginning, people will understand the concept of their ministry's worship. There are some traditions within our culture that are foundational, and that should remain and be taught as such.

"Assimilation" is the process of bringing people into the life of a group. When new members are assimilated into a congregation, they feel a part of the church and begin to experience the church's traditions as their own. They feel the ties that bind them to the common identity of the church, and old members accept and appreciate them. For people to be truly assimilated, both the old and the new members of the church must feel that the new members "belong." All members are then bonded together in their commitment to Christ and by the traditions of a particular church.

---

122 Bruce P. Powers, ed., *Christian Education Handbook* (Nashville: Broadman & Holman, 1996), 256-58.

John Wesley provides a positive example of the assimilation process from church history.

> Wesley's genius lay in his ability to organize seekers and converts into vital discipleship groups called societies, classes, and bands. Each group represented a systematic, progressive step into spiritual maturity. In order to join the Methodist movement a person was first involved for three months in a small group that taught the basics of the faith and discipleship. Then, if the person was willing to submit to accountability and discipline of the cell (which met weekly), one could be recommended for membership. Continued involvement was evaluated quarterly.[123]

The assimilation of members into the Christian community has been a challenge from the beginning. Paul chastised the Corinthians for their divided loyalties and failure to "be united in the same mind and the same purpose" in the company of Christ (1 Cor. 1:10 NRSV). Through much of the church's history, people were considered assimilated by being of "the same mind and judgment" doctrinally and by participating in the worship and rites of their tradition without deviating into heresy.

As a body we must make sure that we have come together in this venue of worship. The lack of unity regarding the concept of worship can cause people not to feel a part of the body, and true assimilation has not taken place until people feel they belong. Assimilation occurs not when people attend church services and events or even when they join the church by confessing or reaffirming a commonly held faith. It happens when they feel that they belong and have become fully accepted and active parts of the body. It once took place because people grew up in a church, and its traditions were their traditions. However, today people

---

123 Michael Slaughter, *Spiritual Entrepreneurs: 6 Principles for Risking Renewal* (Nashville: Abingdon, 1996), 73-74.

move frequently, so new arrivals must be woven into the fabric of the church's community, which can help to develop loyalty to the ministry and revitalize and reconcile worship and other areas of ministry.

This aspect of assimilation is important because the devotional service's spontaneity and praise and worship's sheer joy are both in response to the dynamic movement of the Holy Spirit, which allows worshipers to participate holistically in the worship and to be the spiritual, emotional, intellectual, and physical beings God created them to be.

Denominational Loyalty

Loyalty to the denomination can cause people to hold to the customs and beliefs without any hesitation. While denominational loyalty is decreasing in the United States today, as demonstrated by the many nondenominational ministries springing up across the nation, loyalty can still be found among people within our country. People mostly seek out the type of church or ministry that causes them to feel closest to their beliefs. Within the Pentecostal churches, speaking in tongues or the free expression of spiritual gifts would be an important characteristic. The "gift of the Spirit" has the power to unite persons even from different ethnic and cultural backgrounds. When an area within a denomination becomes flawed or questionable, such as the devotional service within the UHC, this can cause people to begin to discuss the issue in terms of loyalty. The one area within the United Holy Church that weakens loyalty is the inability to discuss differences without dividing or erecting barriers between us. Contemporary praise and worship can deteriorate the fabric of loyalty within the UHC body, because traditional devotional worshipers are holding onto the style of worship upon which the denomination was founded. Therefore, as a body we must teach that these two different types or styles of worship can blend and live together in our denomination, giving God the worship He rightly deserves and desires. When the denomination stands and outlines the guidelines for the revitalization of devotional worship, men and women will accept the instructions and hold to their loyalty to the body.

Acceptance

For a variety of reasons, some people do not feel accepted in the churches of their own families. This is especially true today with the changing of dress codes for worship. At one time women were not allowed to enter the church with pants, but today's culture has no issue with dress codes, because it truly embodies the "come-as-you-are" concept. The church that welcomes with open arms people dealing with issues or those dressed differently will be of a different culture or will be braced for internal struggle. But there must be some acceptance somewhere within the church, because the gospel comes to heal and to set free all mankind regardless of how they dress or look or what they are dealing with. Likewise, believers today must learn to accept different styles of worship and recognize that it has no effect on who God is and what He is capable of doing in the midst of the church. The thing that does hinder Him is the inability to present to him a community of worshipers who stand together in their worship toward Him.

In order for revitalization to occur within the UHC, we must accept individuals and not look at them as blasphemers because they prefer contemporary worship over traditional, devotional services. It is the hope of every worshiper to want his or her style to be accepted, and it is only fair, appropriate, and justified if both groups can accept the other's form of worship.

Justice Oriented

There are people from across the spectrum of society who are convinced that the biblical mandate to strive for justice and peace on this earth requires people to cross boundaries, to negotiate differences, and to work toward a sense of well-being for all. There are certain groups that totally disavow the assimilation process and rather seek both the richness and the challenge of sharing their faith journeys with persons whose spiritual paths are rooted in languages and soils and rituals and prayers of a different generation. They want to be changed by the interchange, to be reformed by new insights, to be inspired by new rhythms and songs.

Our church must sense the urgency. If UHC worshipers cannot learn how to be truly diverse in the church—each person shaping the other and creating a common blend from the mix—they cannot expect peace across the UHC denomination or justice across denominational lines, let alone the world. People join our congregations expecting that their presence will make a difference, that they will challenge some of the status quo, that their heritage will affect some of the power dynamics in the church, and that their expressions of spirituality will influence the form and content of worship. Again, revitalization and reconciliation of worship within the United Holy Church can take place with justice being rendered on both sides. UHC worshipers must remember the words of Amos 5:23-24: "Stop your noisy songs; I do not want to listen to your harps. Instead, let justice flow like a stream, and righteousness like a river that never goes dry."[124] Believers must make sure that justice is released both for those in favor of contemporary praise and worship and for those holding to traditional devotional service.

Conclusion

This work has caused me to look closely at the UHC denomination and see the rich heritage that has been embedded within its fabric from its beginnings. The encounter with twenty-first-century contemporary praise and worship has brought something to the

124 Good News Translation

table that challenged me because of its performance look and because of my own inner feelings. However, I am now truly a lover of praise and worship. During three years of studying biblical worship, I learned that God placed a rich heritage within African American worshipers in the UHC to help them form a worship style that is fitting for them. Everything good that African American believers do as worshipers was first formed in the mind of God and released to the leaders of the United Holy Church and other black church reformations.

Now that we have walked the land and seen the fruit and the giants, it is time to put everything into perspective. Where do we go from here? How do we start? What should be our priorities as pastors and worship leaders? Answers to such questions must be determined in our own hearts by the Spirit of God in the light of His call upon us and what He has revealed to us.

Changes begin with leadership and filter through to the people. The principles in this study should be allowed to challenge our personal lives. God wants to start by turning church leaders into worshipers. When we as leaders begin to live the life of worship, our people will follow.

We must also give immediate attention to the relationship between devotional worship and contemporary praise and worship. So long as differences in philosophy exist between these two, or an impasse in communication presides, congregational worship will continue to be hampered by frustration and stagnation. Devotional service and praise and worship must be blended. It is vital to impart this blended mentality to the devotion leaders and/or praise and worship leaders presently functioning. To the best of our ability, we must build a blending from the potential at our disposal, sharing the ministry of worship among a group of dedicated worshipers from both styles.

Once a blended worship begins to function, we must meet with the people regularly for prayer and the sharing of our spiritual vision for devotional service and praise and worship. We can begin to talk about our goals for the worship services and the faithfulness of God to true worshipers. Also, we need to let the worshipers know that both styles allow one to enter into the presence of God and that both styles can speak to the pain and heartfelt needs of a worshiper. However, the timing and implementation of a particular style are crucial to meeting the needs of worshipers; therefore, worship leaders must be in tune with God to determine the appropriate style at the appropriate time.

Specific services can be discussed, with training offered for a fuller release in the people. Ideas stimulated from the Scriptures on worship should be explored, with specific ideas of implementation examined. We will profit greatly from the strength of a nucleus that is committed to seeing God's will fulfilled in our corporate worship.

Our constant pursuit of God and his purposes should ever cause us to ask for divine guidance and wisdom to know how and where to lead the people He has entrusted to us. Thus we can embark on the glorious and exciting adventure of exploring the uncharted territories of devotional service, which allows one to embrace the hope found during the time of suffering, blended with praise and worship. Together, both styles will lead the congregation into a shared experience that God intends to reveal to His church in the momentous days just ahead.

I close by reaching back into the history of slavery to the words of W. E. B. Dubois, who shared how everything about the black man was stripped from him so that he would easily conform to the views of his master. This same type of stripping of the black male took place through the use of the Willie Lynch Letter in 1712 (attached as Appendix B). With that view in mind, African-Americans continue today, even within our worship services, to seek a style that we feel will speak to who we are and what we are; so we run with haste to anything new. We also reach with anticipation and hope toward new fads and sometimes gimmicks to fill the empty chambers within our souls that hunger for more of God.

Music in African American churches must draw from the heritage of "Negro spirituals" and from traditions that formed a stable bridge to deliver our forebears to safety.[125] Also, it should include evangelical hymns popular in black church experience and traditional and contemporary gospel songs, because music does move the soul. This might be explained by professor of ministry, Robert E. Webber, in his book, *Worship Old & New:* "Music in worship draws the earthly worshiper into the heavens to stand with the heavenly throng as they offer praise to God."[126] We should strive to meet that goal without allowing a war to enter into our sacred space and time and waste another sacred day.

The UHC must be convinced that it is time to offer worship so profoundly nourishing that it will transcend the ever-present messages of the materialist culture and nourish needy spirits. When African Americans recall our ancestors' survival of slavery and the oppression they endured, we have to believe that their survival and sanity was in large part due to the guidance and healing of worship, where the Holy Spirit literally healed and empowered. I am also convinced that we must enhance our already significant usage of the Western mental safeguards and healthy critiques. In fact, what the survey shows about the UHC worshipers is a developing in worship and a drawing closer and closer together—an enriched merger of traditions and a growing knowledge that authentic culture is not instantly manipulable. If the UHC is to be saved from its present precipitous spiritual decline, it will have to be because UHC believers and leaders have used all the spiritual resources God has provided. And that demands the very best of all of the UHC and *all* our cultural and theological traditions and resources. May it please God to cause this to happen soon! Soli Deo Gloria!

---

125 C. Eric Lincoln and Lawrence H. Mamiya, *The Black Church in the African American Experience* (Durham: Duke University Press, 2001), 350.

126 Webber, *Worship Old & New*, 195.

APPENDIX A

REVITALIZATION AND RECONCILIATION OF UHC WORSHIP SURVEY

Section One:

Please answer the following survey questions. Some of the questions are optional, so don't feel pressured to answer. Thank you in advance.

NAME: _____ (optional)

AGE: _____ Male/Female _____ Race _____

Marital Status: M_____ S _____ How Many in Family _____

Occupation: _____

Name of Local Church: _____

How Many Years Have You Been a Member? _____

Are you a tither to your local ministry? _____

Section Two:

Please use this section as a guide or basis for dialogue about your theological understanding of the following Christian basic beliefs. If you need more space for comments, please use the reverse side of this sheet or attach additional pages.

1. How do we know God?

   Answer: _____

   _____

   _____

   _____

   _____

   _____

   _____

2. Explain the incarnation of Christ.

   Answer: _____

   _____

   _____

   _____

   _____

   _____

3. Who is the Holy Ghost?

   Answer: _____

   _____

   _____

   _____

4. What is sin?

Answer: _____

_____

_____

_____

_____

5. What does salvation mean?

Answer: _____

_____

_____

_____

_____

6. List any religious training you may have and how often you attend Bible study at your local ministry.

_____

_____

_____

_____

7. Briefly describe your initial spiritual encounter with your local ministry. How was your worship experience then compared to now?

_____

_____

_____

_____

_____

_____

Section Three:

Please answer the following survey questions by circling the answer that best describes your opinion. Thank you in advance.

1. How satisfied are you with devotional-style worship?

    (Very satisfied, Satisfied, Neutral, Dissatisfied, Very dissatisfied)

2. How satisfied are you with contemporary-style praise and worship?

    (Very satisfied, Satisfied, Neutral, Dissatisfied, Very dissatisfied)

3. Please rate devotional-style worship service and congregation/worship community involvement.

    (Excellent, Good, Average, Fair, Poor)

4. Please rate contemporary-style (praise and worship) worship service and congregation/worship community involvement.

    (Excellent, Good, Average, Fair, Poor)

5. Devotional-style worship provides congregational/community involvement.

    (Strongly agree, Agree, Neutral, Disagree, Strongly Disagree)

6. Contemporary praise-and-worship-style worship provides congregational/community involvement.

    (Strongly agree, Agree, Neutral, Disagree, Strongly Disagree)

7. How often does devotional-style worship service exceed expectations?

   (Very frequently, Frequently, Not Sure, Infrequently, Very Infrequently)

8. How often does contemporary praise-and-worship-style worship service exceed expectations?

   (Very frequently, Frequently, Not Sure, Infrequently, Very Infrequently)

9. To what extent does devotional-style worship service exceed expectations?

   (To very great extent, to great extent, to some extent, to little extent, to very little extent)

10. To what extent does contemporary praise-and-worship-style worship service exceed expectations?

    (To very great extent, to great extent, to some extent, to little extent, to very little extent)

PLEASE GIVE A BRIEF STATEMENT ON THE PROS AND CONS OF THE USE OF THESE STYLES OF WORSHIP IN TODAY'S MINISTRIES.

APPENDIX B

THE WILLIE LYNCH LETTER–1712

GENTLEMAN:

I greet you here on the bank of the James River in the year of our Lord, one thousand seven hundred and twelve. First I shall thank you, the Gentlemen of the Colony of Virginia, for bringing me here. I am here to help you solve some of your problems with slaves. Your invitation reached me on my modest plantation in the West Indies where I have experimented with some of the newest and still the oldest methods for control of slaves. Ancient Rome would envy us if my program is implemented. As our boat sailed south on the James River, named for our illustrious King James, whose bible we cherish, I saw enough to know that your program is not unique. While Rome used cords of wood as crosses for standing human bodies along the old highways in great numbers, you are here using the tree and the rope on occasion.

I caught the whiff of a dead slave hanging from a tree a couple of miles back. You are not only losing valuable stock by hangings, you are having uprisings, slaves are running away, your crops are sometimes left in the fields too long for maximum profit, you suffer occasional fires, your animals are killed, gentlemen...you know what your problems are; I do not need to elaborate. I am not here to enumerate your problems; I am here to introduce you to a method of solving them.

In my bag here, I have a fool-proof method for controlling your black slaves. I guarantee every one of you that if installed correctly it will control the slaves for at least 300 years. My method is simple, any member of your family or any overseer can use it.

I have outlined a number of differences among the slaves, and I take these differences and make them bigger. I use fear, distrust, and envy for control purposes. These methods have worked on my modest plantation in the West Indies, and it will work throughout the South. Take this simple little test of differences and think about them. On the top of my list is "Age", but it is there because it only starts with an "A"; the second is "Color" or shade; there is intelligence, size, sex, size of plantations, attitude of owners, whether the slaves live in the valley, on a hill, East, West, North, South, have fine or coarse hair, or is tall or short. Now that you have a list of differences, I shall give you an outline of action--but before that, I shall assure you that distrust is stronger than trust, and envy is stronger than adulation, respect, or admiration.

The Black Slave, after receiving this indoctrination, shall carry on and will become self refueling and self generating for hundreds of years, maybe thousands.

Don't forget, you must pitch the old Black male vs. the young Black male, and the young Black male against the old Black male. You must use the dark skinned slave's vs. the light skinned slaves, and the light skinned slaves vs. the dark skinned slaves. You must use the female vs. the male, and the male vs. the female. You must also have your servants and overseers distrust all Blacks, but it is necessary that your slaves trust and depend on us. They must love, respect, and trust only us.

Gentlemen, these kits are your keys to control, use them. Have your wives and children use them. Never miss opportunity. My plan is guaranteed, and the good thing about this plan is that if used intensely for one year, the slaves themselves will remain perpetually distrustful.[127]

---

127 Willie Lynch, "The Making of a Slave," http://www.itsabouttimebpp.com/
BPP_Books/pdf/The_Willie_Lynch_Letter_The_Making_Of_A_Slave!.pdf

Bibliography

Aghahowa, Brenda Eatman. *Praising in Black and White: Unity and Diversity in Christian Worship.* Cleveland: United Church Press, 1996.

Barnes, Albert. *Barnes' Notes on the Bible.* E-Sword computer program.

Bartleman, Frank. *Azusa Street—The Roots of Modern-day Pentecost.* Plainfield, NJ: Logos, 1980.

Bell, John L. *The Singing Thing: A Case for Congregational Song.* GIA Publications, 2000.

Black, Kathy. *Culturally Conscious Worship.* St. Louis: Chalice, 2000.

Carson, D. A. *Worship by the Book.* Grand Rapids: Zondervan, 2002.

Cone, James H. "Sanctification, Liberation, and Black Worship." *Theology Today* (July 1978): 139-52.

Cone, James H., and Gayraud S. Wilmore, eds. *Black Theology: A Documentary History - Volume I 1966-1979.* Maryknoll, NY: Orbis, 1993.

Dawn, Marva. *Reaching Out without Dumbing Down: A Theology of Worship for the Turn-of-the-Century Culture.* Grand Rapids: Eerdmans, 1995.

Doran, Carol, and Thomas H. Troeger. *Trouble at the Table: Gathering the Tribes for Worship.* Nashville: Abingdon, 1992.

Du Bois, W. E. B.. *The Souls of Black Folk.* New York: Fawcett, 1961.

Evans, James H., Jr. *We Have Been Believers: An African-American Systematic Theology.* Minneapolis: Fortress, 1992.

Fanon, Frantz. *Black Skin, White Masks.* New York: Grove Press, 1967.

Fee, Gordon D., and Douglas Stuart. *How to Read the Bible for All Its Worth: A Guide to Understanding the Bible.* Grand Rapids: Zondervan, 1993.

Fisher, Henry L. *The History of the United Holy Church of America, Inc.* Durham: privately printed, 1945.

Gallagher, Sally K. "Building Traditions: Comparing Space, Ritual, and Community." *Review of Religious Research,* 47:1 (2005): 70-85.

Gibson, Scott M. *Preaching for Special Services.* Grand Rapids: Baker, 2001.

Gregory, Chester W. *The History of the United Holy Church of America, Inc. 1886-2000.* Baltimore: Gateway, 2000.

Hawn, Michael G. *Gather into One: Praying and Singing Globally.* Grand Rapids: Eerdmans, 2002.

Kaufmann, Walter. *Existentialism From Dostoevsky to Sartre.* New York: New American Library, 1975.

Kimball, Dan, David Crowder, and Sally Morgenthaler. *Emerging Worship: Creating Worship Gatherings for New Generations.* Grand Rapids: Zondervan, 2004.

Lincoln, C. Eric, and Lawrence H. Mamiya. *The Black Church in the African American Experience.* Durham: Duke University Press, 2001.

Malefyt, Norma deWaal, and Howard Vanderwell. *Designing Worship Together: Modes and Strategies for Worship Planning.* Herndon, VA: The Alban Institute, 2005.

Maynard-Reid, Pedrito U. *Diverse Worship: African-American, Caribbean & Hispanic Perspectives.* Downers Grove, IL: InterVarsity, 2000.

McAdoo, Harriette Pipes, ed. *Black Families.* Thousand Oaks, CA: Sage, 1997.

McClung, L. Grant, Jr., ed. *Azusa Street and Beyond: Pentecostal Missions and Church Growth in the Twentieth Century.* South Plainfield, NJ: Bridge, 1986.

Oswalt, John N. Called to Be Holy: A Biblical Perspective. Nappanee, IN: Evangel, 1999,

Palmer, Albert W. *The Art of Conducting Public Worship.* New York: Macmillan, 1953.

Parrett, Gary. "Culturrally Relevant." D.Min. course notes, *Gordon-Conwell Theological seminary,* 2008.

Payne, Wardell J. *Directory of African American Religious Bodies.* 2nd ed. Washington, DC: Howard University Press, 1995.

Peterson, David. *Engaging With God: A Biblical Theology of Worship.* Downers Grove, IL: InterVarsity, 1992.

Peterson, Eugene H. *The Message: The Bible in Contemporary Language.* Colorado Springs: NavPress, 2002.

Plantinga, Cornelius, Jr., and Sue A. Rozeboom. *Discerning the Spirits: A Guide to Thinking about Christian Worship Today.* Grand Rapids: Eerdmans, 2003.

Powers, Bruce P., ed. *Christian Education Handbook.* Nashville: Broadman & Holman, 1996.

Slaughter, Michael. Spiritual Entrepreneurs: 6 Principles for Risking Renewal. Nashville: Abingdon, 1996.

Spencer, Jon Michael. *Sing a New Song: Liberating Black Hymnody.* Minneapolis: Fortress, 1995.

Turner, William C., Jr. *The United Holy Church of America.* Piscataway, NJ: Georgias, 2006.

Webber, Robert E. *Planning Blended Worship: The Creative Mixture of Old and New.* Nashville: Abingdon, 1998.

———. *Worship Is a Verb: Eight Principles for Transforming Worship.* Peabody, MA: Hendrickson, 1995.

———. *Worship Old & New: A Biblical, Historical, and Practical Introduction.* Grand Rapids: Zondervan, 1994.

Wesley, John. *Wesley's Explanatory Notes on the Whole Bible.* E-Sword computer program.

White, James F. *The Brief History of Christian Worship.* Nashville: Abingdon, 1993.

Wikipedia. "Church of the Brethren." http://en.wikipedia.org/wiki/Church_of_the_Brethren.

Wikipedia. "Josefina de Vasconcellos." http://en.wikipedia.org/wiki/Josefina_de_Vasconcellos.

Willard, Dallas. *Renovation of the Heart: Putting on the Character of Christ.* Colorado Springs: NavPress, 2002.

Wilmore, Gayraud S. *Black Religion and Black Radicalism: An Interpretation of the Religious History of African Americans.* Maryknoll, NY: Orbis, 1998.